JN066247

# リテリングを活用した英語指導

*Retelling*

理解した内容を自分の言葉で発信する

佐々木啓成 著

大修館書店

# はじめに

　英語指導では，「読む」,「聞く」,「話す」,「書く」といったバランスの
とれた4技能の育成が求められていますが，この中でも，特に「話す」技
能の育成に費やす時間は少ないように思えます。しかし，近年，検定教科
書を使用しながら「話す」機会を確保できる活動として，リテリングが注
目されています。

　リテリングは母語によるコミュニケーションにおいても頻繁に行われま
す。例えば，昨日起こった出来事を話したり，これまでに経験したことの
ある出来事について話したりすることは日常的に行われる行為です。この
ことからも，英語指導にリテリングを取り入れることはコミュニケーショ
ン能力を伸長させるのに有益であることが分かります。本書の中でも解説
をしますが，リテリングという言葉はリプロダクションという言葉と混同
されて使われることがあるので，本書では，リプロダクションを「再生活
動」,リテリングを「再生活動＋産出活動」,ディベートやディスカッショ
ンなどの即興的活動を「産出活動」として使い分けます。

　検定教科書を使用した指導では，リーディングやリスニングといった受
容技能に焦点が当てられることが多く，スピーキングやライティングと
いった産出技能に対する指導時間が少ない，あるいは，全く行われない
といった状況が見られました。そのような状況において，本文の内容につい
て話したり，書いたりする活動であるリテリングを導入することによって，
産出技能の指導時間を増やすことができ，4技能統合型の授業実践が可能
となります。しかし，英語習熟度の低い生徒にとって，リテリングは負荷
の高い活動であり，授業中で行うことに抵抗感を持つ教師も少なからずお
られるように思います。そこで，本書では，あらゆる英語習熟度を持つ生
徒に対してリテリング指導を行うことができるように，認知負荷を考慮し
て段階的に指導できる方法について解説をしており，指導例として複数の

異なるレベルの検定教科書を使用しました。

　本書を通じて，リテリングに関する知見やリテリングを成功させるための指導方法を学び，指導する生徒の英語習熟度に応じたリテリング指導の実践力を身に付けることができ，日々の指導に新たな変化が生まれるなら幸いです。

　2020年7月

佐々木啓成

# 目　次

# リテリングを活用した英語指導

## 理解した内容を自分の言葉で発信する

# 第1章
# リテリングとは何か

## 1.1　なぜリテリングは有益なのか

　リテリングとは，読んだり，聞いたりしたことを，何らかの補助的なメモ等を見ながら，第3者に伝える活動です。リテリングは「re + telling」ですが，*Longman Dictionary of Contemporary English*（6th Edition）には，"to give information to somebody by speaking or writing" と記載されていることからも，本書では，リテリングには，「話す」以外に「書く」という手段も存在するという立場を取っています。

　卯城（2009）では，リテリングの利点をいくつか述べています。まず，リテリングを行うことで，本文の内容理解を中心とした「教師主導型」で行われてきた従来型のリーディング指導を「生徒主導型」の活動に変えることができると述べています。次に，リテリングは本文の内容に接触する頻度を高めると述べています。リテリングは基本的にはペアで行うことが多く，ペアでリテリングを行うときには，①ペアによるリテリングの準備練習として個人でリテリングをする，②自分がペアの相手に向かってリテリングをする，③ペアの相手のリテリングを聞く，といったように1セットで少なくとも3回は本文の内容に触れることになります。さらに，リテリングは読解を深める効果があるとも述べています。リテリングを行うときには，本文の内容を相手が分かるように伝えなければならないので，頭の中で情報を整理する必要があり，このプロセスが読解プロセスと類似していると説明しています。以上のことから，リテリングは，「読解を深めながら，生徒たちが主体的に取り組めるアウトプット活動」と考えること

ができます。

　文部科学省が報告した「平成29年度英語力調査結果（高校3年生）」において，CEFR（ヨーロッパ言語共通参照枠）A2レベル以上の生徒の割合は「読むこと」で33.5%，「聞くこと」で33.6%，「話すこと」で12.9%，「書くこと」で19.7%という結果が出ています。特に「話すこと」と「書くこと」のレベルは全体的に低く，無得点者の割合もそれぞれ18.8%と15.1%と一定数いる状況であり，アウトプット量が少ない指導における課題が浮き彫りとなっています。近年，バランスの取れた4技能の育成が求められる中で，アウトプット技能を伸長させるためには，話したり，書いたりする機会を可能な限り多く与えることが必要であり，本文の内容を英語で話したり，書いたりするリテリングはそれを実現できる有益な活動です。

　別の調査であるベネッセ教育総合研究所による「中高の英語指導に関する実態調査2015」では，中学校で73.7%，高等学校で74.4%が「コミュニケーション能力の育成と，入試のための指導を両立させることが難しい」と回答していますが，リテリングを授業内で行うことで，インプット技能とアウトプット技能の育成を両立させることができます。また，「生徒が英語を使う言語活動を行う」という質問項目に対して，中学校で35.6%，高等学校で19.0%しか「十分実行している」と回答していません。これは，授業内における英語による言語活動が不十分であることを示唆しており，リテリングはその割合を上げる方策の1つになります。さらに，「4技能のバランスを考慮して指導する」という質問項目に対しては，中学校で15.3%，高等学校で9.8%しか「十分実行している」と回答しておらず，国が求める4技能統合型の授業実践の少なさを示唆しています。これらの課題に対しても，本文を読んだり，聞いたりした後に，その内容についてリテリングをし，仕上げとして本文の内容について即興的な自己表現活動を行うなどの指導は，その解決策の1つとなります。

　現在，学校現場における英語指導の課題は数多くありますが，上述したように多くの利点があるリテリングは，課題のいくつかを解決できる活動であると考えられます。

## 1.2 リテリングにはどのような種類があるのか

リテリングには，以下のように2つの種類があります。

（1）初見のまとまりのある英文を読ませた後に，その内容についてリテリングをさせることで，内容理解度を測るテストとして利用されるもの。質問項目の難易度などの影響を受けないという点において，読解力を測定できると言われています（Lee, 1986 ; Alderson, 2000）。

（2）本文の内容理解を終えた後に行い，その内容についてリテリングをさせることで，言語表現のインテイク活動やアウトプット活動として利用されるもの（山本，1998 ; 池邊，2004）。

（1）は，学校現場ではほとんど行われないリテリングの種類です。これはどちらかと言うと，読解力の測定を目的として研究者によって使用されるものです。中学校・高等学校教師がリテリングを行うときは，（2）を目的としたものになるでしょう。本書で扱うリテリングという言葉も，後者の種類を指します。

## 1.3 第二言語習得の認知プロセスを理解しよう

リテリングを取り入れた指導について考える前に，村野井（2006）が提案する第二言語習得の認知プロセスに関するモデルを紹介します。このモデルでは，インプットからアウトプットまでの流れを以下のように示しています。

1 インプット（input）
2 気づき（noticing）
3 理解（comprehension）
4 内在化（intake）
5 統合（integration）

6　アウトプット（output）

「1　インプット（input）」とは，文字や音声を媒体として，語彙，文法，音などが耳に入ってくることです。

「2　気づき（noticing）」とは，生徒が文字や音声を媒体として，語彙，文法，音などに気づくことです。理解をするかどうかは別の問題で，生徒が文字や音声に注意を払いさえすれば，この段階を経ることができます。

「3　理解（comprehension）」とは，前段階で注意を払った言語材料を意味とつなげ，そして，それらの機能を理解することであり，「形式・意味・機能マッピング（form-meaning-function mapping）」を行うことと言い換えることができます。日本語による文法説明と日本語訳の確認が中心の従来型の指導では，この段階に至ることが目標となります。

「4　内在化（intake）」とは，「形式・意味・機能マッピング」を行った後に，それらの理解を一時的なものに留めるのではなく，定着を目指す段階です。例えば，学校現場における指導としては，音読活動を通じて，本文に出てきた言語材料を取り込む段階と考えられます。

「5　統合（integration）」とは，内在化した言語材料が自動的，瞬間的に使えるように長期記憶に貯蔵されるプロセスです。

「6　アウトプット（output）」とは，実際に目標言語を話したり，書いたりして使用することを意味します。

## 1.4　リテリングとリプロダクションの違いとは

リテリング（retelling）は，リプロダクション（reproduction）とも呼ばれることがあり，これら2つの言葉は混同して使われています。この2つの言葉に境界線を引くために，発話される英語の質という観点からこれらの活動について考えてみます。

リテリングを行うときには，生徒が発話する英語の質は大きく2つに分けられます。1つ目は，本文の言語形式を自分の言葉に言い換えたもので，いわゆる，パラフレーズと呼ばれるものです。2つ目は，本文と同じ，あるいはほぼ同じ言語形式で再生されたものです。これら2つの異なる英語

の質を「リテリング」と「リプロダクション」という言葉に落とし込もうとするときの手がかりとして，"retell" と "reproduce" を *Longman Dictionary of Contemporary English*（6th Edition）で調べてみると，以下の定義が記載されています。

retell

*to tell a story again, often in a different way or in a different language*

reproduce

*to make something happen in the same way as it happened before*

上記の定義から，以下のように整理をしました。

| リテリング<br>（retelling） | リプロダクション<br>（reproduction） |
|---|---|
| 本文の言語形式を自分の言葉に<br>言い換えたもの | 本文と同じ，あるいはほぼ同じ<br>言語形式で再生されたもの |

表1-1　リテリングとリプロダクションの違い

　次に，これら2つを認知プロセスに関するモデルに適用させようとすると，リテリングもリプロダクションも，本文の内容について英文を見ないで，実際に話したり，書いたりする活動なので，アウトプットとみなすことができそうです。しかし，リプロダクションにおける発話の質は，本文と同じ，あるいはほぼ同じ言語形式で再生されたものなので，完全なアウトプットとは言い切れないようにも思えます。むしろ，文字を見ない音読と呼べるのかもしれません。音読は，フレーズあるいは文を単位として，言語材料をそのままの形で長期記憶へ取り込む活動です。門田（2012）は，鈴木（2005）を引用して，音読には，「音声と文字を結びつけるための音読」と「語彙や文法規則を内在化させるための音読」があると述べています。このことからも，「音読活動＝内在化」と考えることができそうです

し，長期記憶への貯蔵ということで言うと，「統合」とも考えられるのかもしれません。実際の指導に「内在化」と「統合」という言葉を落とし込むのがなかなか難しそうです。しかし，文字を見て行う音読より，文字を見ずに再生するリプロダクションの方が認知負荷の高い活動であることは間違いないでしょう。また，本文と同じ，あるいはほぼ同じ言語形式で再生されるリプロダクションより，本文の言語形式を自分の言葉に言い換えるリテリングの方が認知負荷は高いと言えるでしょう。

　以上のことを考慮して「音読」，「リプロダクション」，「リテリング」を再整理しようとすると，やはり，「内在化」と「統合」を区別する難しさに悩みます。そこで，本書では，本文にある理解した言語材料の取り込みである「内在化」と，内在化した言語材料が自動的，瞬間的に使えるように長期記憶に貯蔵されるプロセスである「統合」を1つにまとめて「内在化」と呼ぶことにします。また，整理するときに，本文の言語材料を用いたリプロダクション，あるいは，本文の言語形式を自分の言葉に言い換えるリテリングよりもさらに認知負荷の高いアウトプットである自己表現活動も組み入れることにしました。そうやって整理したのが，「音読」，「リプロダクション」，「リテリング」，「自己表現」を軸とした以下の指導モデルです。

| 形式重視 | | 形式＋意味重視 | 意味重視 |
|---|---|---|---|
| インテイク | アウトプットⅠ | アウトプットⅡ | アウトプットⅢ |
| 内在化 | 再生 | 再生＋産出 | 産出 |
| 音読 | リプロダクション | リテリング | 自己表現 |

**認知負荷が低い** ————————————————————————▶ **認知負荷が高い**

表1-2　リテリングを取り入れた指導モデル

　この指導モデルでは，活動を音読，リプロダクション，リテリング，自己表現の4種類に分け，それぞれの活動を3つの観点で分類しました。1つ目は，「形式重視」，「形式＋意味重視」，「意味重視」のように「何を重視した活動なのか」という観点で分類をしました。2つ目は，第二言語習

得における認知プロセスの大きな枠組みである「インプット→インテイク→アウトプット」で分類をしました。「アウトプット」を認知負荷に応じて，「アウトプットⅠ」，「アウトプットⅡ」，「アウトプットⅢ」に分けました。数字が増えるにつれて，負荷が大きくなります。3つ目は「内在化」，「再生」，「再生＋産出」，「産出」のように「活動の目的は何であるのか」という観点で分類をしました。このように整理することで，音読から自己表現までの全体的な流れと認知負荷の高低が明確になり，指導するときの有益なモデルになると考えました。音読やリプロダクションは，「内在化」や「再生」を目的とする活動ですが，それに留まらずに「産出」を加えることを授業の目標とするならば，あるいは，「形式」だけでなく，「意味」も重視するならば，リテリングを目指すべきであることが可視化できます。

　本書では，章のタイトルや指導例等に対して，発話の質によって呼び方の異なる「リテリング」と「リプロダクション」を使い分けるのが難しいので，本文の内容について話したり，書いたりする活動を基本的に「リテリング」と呼び，特に，発話の質について言及しなければならないときに，「リプロダクション」という言葉を使用しています。また，「リテリング」という言葉を使用するときには，口頭によるリテリングと，筆記によるリテリングの両方を意味することがあり，たとえ，口頭によるリテリングに言及していても，それは筆記によるリテリングにも適用できる場合があると考えてください。

## 1.5　リテリングの手順

　ここでは検定教科書を使用してリテリングを行う手順について解説をします。手順は以下のように5つあります。それぞれの手順における具体的な指導については第2章以降で解説していきます。

（Ⅰ）内容理解［→第2章］
（Ⅱ）音読による内在化［→第3章］
（Ⅲ）発話情報の選定［→第4章］

（Ⅳ）英語への変換 ［→第5章］
（Ⅴ）発話 ［→第6章］

　リテリング指導を成功させるためには，まずは本文を理解し，音読によって本文の言語材料を内在化させることが重要です。次に，本文中の要点だけを発話するのか，あるいは，細部情報も発話するのかといったように，発話情報を選定しなければなりません。さらに，リプロダクション（本文と同じ，あるいはほぼ同じ言語形式での再生）を目指すのか，リテリング（本文の言語形式を自分の言葉に言い換える）を目指すのかも考えなければなりません。最後は，それを正確に発声できるかです。また，（Ⅴ）発話にはどのような形態で発話させるのかという観点も含まれています。次の章からは，上記にあるリテリングの手順に沿って，具体的に指導の解説をします。

## 第1章のまとめ

- リテリングには，「リーディング指導を生徒主導型の活動に変えることができる」，「本文の内容に接触する頻度を高める」，「読解を深める効果がある」といった利点がある。

- 「平成29年度英語力調査結果（高校3年生）」の結果から，「話すこと」と「書くこと」に課題が見られる。

- 「中高の英語指導に関する実態調査2015」の結果から，コミュニケーション能力の育成と，入試のための指導を両立させることや，4技能のバランスを考慮して指導することに課題を感じている教師が多い。

- リテリングには，「内容理解度を測るテストとして利用されるもの」と「言語表現のインテイク活動やアウトプット活動として利用されるもの」の2つの種類があるが，授業で行われるリテリングは後者である。

- 第二言語習得の認知プロセスには，インプット，気づき，理解，内在化，統合，アウトプットがある。

- リテリングは，「本文の言語形式を自分の言葉に言い換えたもの」であり，リプロダクションは，「本文と同じ，あるいはほぼ同じ言語形式で再生されたもの」であり，両者には違いがある。

- 音読には，「音声と文字を結びつけるための音読」と「語彙や文法規則を内在化させるための音読」がある。

- 本書が提案する指導モデルでは，活動を音読，リプロダクション，リテリング，自己表現の4種類に分け，それぞれの活動を「形式と意味」，「インテイクとアウトプット」，「内在化と再生と産出」といった3つの観点で分類をした。

- リテリングの手順には，「内容理解」，「音読による内在化」，「発話情報の選定」，「英語への変換」，「発話」がある。

# 第2章
# リテリングの手順（Ⅰ）：内容理解

　リテリングをするときには本文の内容を理解することが不可欠です。内容理解が十分でないと、当然、伝えるべき内容が曖昧になり、相手にうまく伝えることができません。では、内容理解はリスニングとリーディングのどちらで行うのがよいのでしょうか。4技能統合型の授業実践が求められる近年の英語指導においては、リスニング量の確保という観点からも、閉本状態でリスニングによる内容理解を行うことが必要です。内容理解はリスニングからリーディングの流れで行うのがよいでしょう。

　内容理解後に行うリテリングでは、まずは「要点」を伝えることができるようになってから、「要点」に「細部情報」を追加して伝える流れがよいでしょう。よって、内容理解も「要点」から「細部情報」へと理解する流れにします。桃山学院教育大学の鈴木寿一先生が提唱するラウンド制指導法（ジャパンライム株式会社（2017））における内容理解では、「概要→要点→細部」の順に理解する方法を推奨しており、ラウンド制指導法を用いることでリテリングにつながる内容理解を行うことができます。

## 2.1　ラウンド制指導法における内容理解の手順

　以下に、ラウンド制指導法における内容理解の手順を示します（※は補足内容です）。

（1）パラグラフ数に応じて、本文に関する質問を与えます。
　　※質問形式はTF問題だと消去法で答えることができる可能性があるので、
　　記述で答えさせる質問形式が好ましいです。

※生徒の英語習熟度に応じて，日本語で答えさせるのか，英語で答えさせるのかは判断してください。

（2）本文を見ないで，音声を数回聞かせ，与えられた質問に答えさせます。

※質問に答えることと，音声を聞くことを同時に処理するのはかなり負荷が高いので，例えば1パートを扱う場合，パート全体の音声を聞かせるのではなく，パラフラフごとに聞かせ，答える時間を与えます。音声を聞くときには，鉛筆を置かせ，聞くことに集中させます。

（3）テキストを開本させて本文を読ませ，もう一度，同じ質問に答えさせます。

※（2）で音声を聞いたときに，うまく聞けなかった部分については文字を見ることによって，「そういうことだったのか」という気づきが生まれ，音声と文字のつながりを強化できます。

（4）ペアやグループで質問に対する答えを共有し，答えが異なっていれば話し合いをさせます。

※この活動によって協同学習を取り入れることができます。

（5）重要箇所については解説を行ったり，構文指導等を行うことで内容理解をさらに深めさせます。

※全ての文の解説を行う必要はありませんが，特に，構造の複雑な文を取り上げて解説するのがよいでしょう。

（6）本文を見ながら音声を聞かせ，一定のスピードで内容理解をさせます。

※速読力の伸長のためにも，意味のまとまりごとにスラッシュを入れた本文プリントを使用することをお薦めします。

（7）仕上げとして，本文を見ないで音声を聞かせ，音声だけで内容理解をさせます。

※音声を聞かせる回数は生徒の英語習熟度に応じて判断してください。

以下は *Genius English CommunicationI Revised*（大修館書店，平成29年度発行）の LESSON 6　Willpower and Sleep の Part1 を題材とした内容理解プリントの例です。

LESSON 6　Willpower and Sleep

［Part 1］

① Willpower is the important ability to control our attention, emotions, and desires. It influences our lives in many ways. People who use willpower more than others are happier and healthier. If you want to improve your lives, willpower is not a bad place to start.

② In order to find effective ways to develop willpower, we can rely on new insights from science. A number of ways have been found to help us create healthy habits for gaining willpower. Getting good sleep is one of them.

③ We all know that good sleep is important. If you sleep less than six hours a night, there is a good chance you feel your willpower is not strong enough. The bedroom is the most important place where willpower is created. The lack of sleep makes it more difficult to control your emotions, focus your attention, or find the energy to tackle challenges you face. If you do not sleep properly, you may find yourself feeling bad all day. You may blame yourself for having weak willpower. Let's see how getting better sleep can help with these problems.

**【日本語による内容理解プリントの例】**

LESSON 6　Willpower and Sleep

［Part 1］

要点

〈パラグラフ①〉
●なぜ，意志力は重要な能力ですか。
〈パラグラフ②〉
●意志力を得るための1つの方法は何ですか。
〈パラグラフ③〉
●あなたの意志力が十分に強くないと感じさせる原因は何ですか。
●睡眠不足になれば何をすることが困難になりますか。

細部情報
〈パラグラフ①〉
○他の人よりも強く意志力を働かせることであなたはどうなりますか。
〈パラグラフ②〉
○意志力を発達させるための効果的な方法を見つけるのに私たちは何に頼ることができますか。
〈パラグラフ③〉
○意志力が作り出される最も重要な場所はどこですか。
○もしあなたが適切に睡眠をとらなければ，どのように感じますか。

　内容理解のための質問は，「要点」と「細部情報」に分けてあります。これは，リテリングをするときに，「要点」を問う質問の答えをつなぎ合わせると「要点」について話すことができ，また，「要点」に「細部情報」を問う質問の答えを追加して話すことで，より内容の濃いリテリングをすることができるように意図しています。

## 2.2　英問英答をどのように活用するのか

　2.1で紹介した内容理解プリントの例では，日本語による質問を用いましたが，英語による質問を用いて，英語で答えさせる，つまり，英問英答をさせることも考えられます。リテリングに関連する英問英答には，「内容理解のための英問英答」と「即興的な英問英答」の2種類があります。
　「内容理解のための英問英答」は，「英語による内容理解プリント」を使用した指導のことです。「日本語による内容理解プリント」の例でも紹介したように，ここでも「要点」を理解させるものと，「細部情報」を理解させるものに分けておくことでリテリングにつながる内容理解となります。

LESSON 6　Willpower and Sleep

［Part 1］

要点

〈パラグラフ①〉

● Why is willpower an important ability?

〈パラグラフ②〉

● What is one way to gain willpower?

〈パラグラフ③〉

● What makes you feel your willpower is not strong?

● What does the lack of sleep make more difficult?

細部情報

〈パラグラフ①〉

○ What does using willpower more than others make you?

〈パラグラフ②〉

○ What can we rely on to find effective ways to develop willpower?

〈パラグラフ③〉

○ What is the most important place where willpower is created?

○ If you do not sleep properly, how do you feel?

　「即興的な英問英答」は，リテリングを終えた段階で，内容理解度とリテリングの達成度を確認する目的で行うものです。以下はペアによる英問英答プリントの例です。AとBで異なる2種類のプリントを作成します。質問をする側は文字を見て質問を言うのではなく，Read and Look up で言うように指導します（※ Read and Look up の方法については，3.4 を参照）。答える側は可能な限り実際の会話を意識して答えます。例えば，What makes you feel your willpower is not strong? という質問に対して，Sleeping less than six hours a night makes you feel your willpower is not strong. と答えるよりも，Sleeping less than six hours a night does. と答えることを目指します。また，AとBのプリントを交換させて使用することで，すべての質問に答えさせることができます。

LESSON 6  Willpower and Sleep
［Part 1］
要点
〈パラグラフ①〉
● Why is willpower an important ability?
→ Because it can control our attention, emotions, and desires.
〈パラグラフ③〉
● What makes you feel your willpower is not strong?
→ Sleeping less than six hours a night does.

細部情報
〈パラグラフ①〉
○ What does using willpower more than others make you?
→ It makes you happier and healthier.
〈パラグラフ③〉
○ What is the most important place where willpower is created?
→ The bedroom is.

【即興的な英問英答プリントの例（B）】

LESSON 6  Willpower and Sleep
［Part 1］
要点
〈パラグラフ②〉
● What is one way to gain willpower?
→ Getting good sleep is.
〈パラグラフ③〉
● What does the lack of sleep make more difficult?
→ It makes controlling your emotions more difficult.

細部情報
〈パラグラフ②〉
○ What can we rely on to find effective ways to develop willpower?
→ We can rely on new insights from science.

<パラグラフ③>
○ If you do not sleep properly, how do you feel?
→ We may find / ourselves feeling bad all day.

## 2.3 リテリングにつながる語彙指導とは

　語彙には，読んだり，聞いたりするときに，意味を想起できればよい「受容語彙」と，話したり，書いたりするときに使われる「発表語彙」に分類することができます。語彙指導を行うときには，指導の目的が「受容語彙」を増やすための指導であるのか，「発表語彙」を増やすための指導であるのかを区別して指導する必要があります。リテリングは発話を伴う活動ですので語彙指導では，意味の想起に留まらず，使用を目的とするべきです。また，リテリングでは，本文の語彙を使用して話すので，リテリングという活動自体に「発表語彙」を増やす効果があります。

### 2.3.1 語彙リストを用いた語彙指導

　リテリングにつながる語彙指導としては，まずは英語を見て，あるいは聞いて，日本語の想起ができるようにしてから，最終的には日本語を見て，あるいは聞いて，英語を言うことができるように指導するべきです。そのために，語彙リストは，左側に日本語，右側に英語を配置します。ペア活動で使用するならば，生徒Aに日本語を言わせ，生徒Bにその日本語に対応する英語を言わせます。以下は，*Revised LANDMARK English Communication I*（啓林館，平成29年度発行）のLESSON 6 Biodiesel Adventure の Part 1 を題材とした語彙リストの作成例です。この語彙リストでは日本語の一部が空欄になっていますが，これは内容理解のときに生徒に推測をさせたい語彙です。

Lesson 6  Biodiesel Adventure
［Part 1］
　I am Shusei Yamada, a photojournalist. I drove around the world with

"Vasco-5," an eco-friendly car. The car runs on vegetable oil! It carries a machine which makes biodiesel fuel out of used vegetable oil. I did not buy new oil but collected waste oil from people in many countries.

There were two purposes of this adventure. One purpose was to examine how far I could go with only waste oil. The other purpose was to communicate with people around the world about biodiesel fuel.

Before beginning my journey, I had worried about one thing. In the world, there are many varieties of vegetable oils such as rapeseed, palm, and olive oil. I was not sure if Vasco-5 could process all of these oils. But some people say the only way to learn is "by doing." So, I started the engine of Vasco-5 in

| 日本語 | 英語 |
|---|---|
| （名）バイオディーゼル | biodiesel |
| （名）冒険 | adventure |
| （名）報道写真家 | photojournalist |
| （名）バスコファイブ号 | Vasco-5 |
| （形） | eco-friendly |
| （名） | fuel |
| （形）廃物の | waste |
| （動） | examine |
| （名）旅 | journey |
| （名）種類 | variety |
| （名）菜種 | rapeseed |
| （名）ヤシ | palm |
| （名）オリーブ | olive |
| （動） | process |
| （名）エンジン | engine |

Tokyo on December 5th, 2007.

　この語彙リストを用いたペア活動を行う前には，個々の語彙を正確に発音できるように指導することが必要です。以下の指導例のように，Listen and Repeat の後に，Read aloud, Listen and Repeat を行うのがよいでしょう。

**【指導の流れ】**　※ Tは教師　Sは生徒

〈Listen and Repeat〉

T："biodiesel" と発音し，モデルを示す。

S：(モデルをよく聞いて) "biodiesel" と発音する。

T："adventure"

S："adventure"

T："photojournalist"

S："photojournalist"

〈Read aloud, Listen and Repeat〉

T：日本語で「バイオディーゼル」と言う。

S："biodiesel" と発音する。

T："biodiesel" と発音し，モデルを示す。

S：(モデルをよく聞いて) "biodiesel" と発音する。

T：「冒険」

S："adventure"

T："adventure"

S："adventure"

　Read aloud, Listen and Repeat では，自分で発音した後で，教師のモデルを聞いて，自分の発音が正しかったのかを確認した後に，再び発音をするので，正確に発音できるようになります。内容理解のときに推測させたい語彙については，日本語が記載されていないので，教師が日本語を言う部分は省略します。

## 2.3.2 日本語訳を用いた語彙指導

　Listen and Repeat や Read aloud, Listen and Repeat で語彙指導を終え，さらに内容理解を終えた後に，リテリングの準備段階として行う語彙指導を紹介します。以下の日本語訳プリントを見ながら四角で囲まれた語（句）を英語で言わせます。

**【日本語訳プリント】**

> 　私は 報道写真家 の山田周生です。私は 環境に優しい 車「バスコファイブ号」で 世界をドライブして一周 しました。その車は 植物油 で走るのです！その車は 使用済みの植物油 からバイオディーゼル 燃料 を作る機械を 載せて います。私は新しい油を買うのではなく，たくさんの国の人たちから 廃油 を 集めま した。
> 　この 冒険 の目的は2つありました。1つ目の 目的 は， 廃油だけ でどこまで行けるのか 調査 することでした。もう1つの 目的 は， 世界中の人たち とバイオディーゼル燃料について 情報交換 することでした。
> 　 旅 を始める前，私は1つのことについてずっと心配していました。世界には， 菜種油 ， ヤシ油 ， オリーブ油 のように 多くの種類 の 植物油 があります。バスコファイブ号がこれらすべての油を 加工 できるかどうか 確信がなかった のです。しかし， 唯一の学習方法 は「行動することによる」と言う人もいます。だから私は，2007年12月5日，東京でバスコファイブ号のエンジンをかけました。

**【指導の流れ】**　※ペアで2文ごとに交代する場合

S1：私は "photojournalist" の山田周生です。私は "eco-friendly" 車「バスコファイブ号」で "drove around the world" しました。

S2：その車は "vegetable oil" で走るのです！その車は "used vegetable oil" からバイオディーゼル "fuel" を作る機械を "carries" しています。

S1：私は新しい油を買うのではなく，たくさんの国の人たちから "waste oil" を "collected" しました。この "adventure" の "purpose" は2つありました。

S2：1つ目の "purpose" は， "only waste oil" でどこまで行けるのか "examine" することでした。もう1つの "purpose" は， "people around the world" とバイオディーゼル燃料について "communicate" することでした。(以下省略)

### 2.3.3 英英辞典の定義を用いた語彙指導

　この語彙指導もリテリングの準備段階として行うものです。新出語に対して，英語で書かれた定義を提示することでパラフレーズを促すことができます。特にパラフレーズをさせたい語の定義を空欄にして生徒に考えさせます。

| 日本語 | 英語 | 定義 |
|---|---|---|
| （名）バイオディーゼル | biodiesel | a non-petroleum-based diesel fuel made by vegetable oils or animal fats |
| （名）冒険 | adventure | |
| （名）報道写真家 | photojournalist | someone who reports news stories in newspapers and magazines using mainly photographs instead of words |
| （名）バスコファイブ号 | Vasco-5 | |
| （形）環境に優しい | eco-friendly | not harmful to the environment |
| （名）燃料 | fuel | a substance such as coal, gas, or oil that can be burned to produce heat or energy |
| （形）廃物の | waste | waste materials, substances, etc. are unwanted because the good part of them has been removed |
| （動）〜を調査する | examine | |
| （名）旅 | journey | a time spent travelling from one place to another, especially over a long distance |

| （名）種類 | variety | a type of thing that is different from others in the same group |
|---|---|---|
| （名）菜種 | rapeseed | the seed of the rape plant, with yellow flowers |
| （名）ヤシ | palm | a tropical tree which grows near beaches or in deserts, with a long straight trunk and large pointed leaves at the top |
| （名）オリーブ | olive | a small, bitter, egg-shaped black or green fruit, used as food and for making oil |
| （動）加工する | process | to treat raw material in order to change it |
| （名）エンジン | engine | the part of a vehicle that produces power to make the vehicle move |

生徒が考えた定義

〈adventure「冒険」〉

○ Going to unknown places to discover new things or new places

○ Going to some places which we have never been to

○ Going to unknown or dangerous places and discovering new things


〈photojournalist「報道写真家」〉

○ A person who take pictures to tell people the fact

○ A person who go to the place where some accidents happened and take pictures there

○ A person who take pictures to let many people know the news

○ A journalist who tells information with photos

○ A person who tells us what happened all over the world using pictures


〈examine「～を調査する」〉

○ research something

○ investigate something

○ look into things

○ check something which is not clear

○ try to know things that you don't know

○ look at the things carefully

○ try to know more about things that we want to know

## 第２章のまとめ

〈リテリングの手順〉
- （Ⅰ）**内容理解**
- （Ⅱ）音読による内在化
- （Ⅲ）発話情報の選定
- （Ⅳ）英語への変換
- （Ⅴ）発話

● 内容理解は，４技能統合の観点からも，リスニングからリーディングへの流れがよい。初聴で内容理解をさせる場合には，予習を求めない指導になる。

● 本文の情報には，「要点」と「細部情報」があり，内容理解では，「要点」を理解させてから，「細部情報」を理解させる流れで指導するとリテリングにつなげやすい。

● ラウンド制指導法による内容理解はリテリングとの親和性が高く，この指導法では，パラグラフ数に応じて，「要点」と「細部情報」に分けて，本文に関する質問を与える。また，「要点」を問う質問の答えをつなぎ合わせると内容のあるリテリングになるように質問を考える。

● 英問英答には，「内容理解のための英問英答」と「即興的な英問英答」の２種類があり，前者は質問を読んで，筆記で答える形式であ

り，後者はパートナーの質問を聞いて，口頭で答える形式である。

●「内容理解のための英問英答」では，日本語による内容質問と同様
に，質問は「要点」と「細部情報」に分けるのがよい。

●リテリングにつながる語彙指導には，「語彙リストを用いた語彙指
導」があり，リテリングにつながるように「日→英」ができるよう
に指導する。また，内容理解のときに推測させたい語彙について
は，空欄にしておくのがよい。

●リテリングの準備段階での語彙指導法としては，「日本語訳を用い
た語彙指導」がある。この指導では，本文の内容を確認しながら，
新出語彙の「日→英」の完成度を確認できる。

●パラフレーズを促す語彙指導として，「英英辞典の定義を用いた語
彙指導」がある。生徒たちに自由に英語で定義を考えさせるのがよ
い。また，英英辞典の使用を促すことにもなる。

## 第3章

# リテリングの手順（Ⅱ）：
# 音読による内在化

　既述しましたが，門田（2012）は，鈴木（2005）を引用して，音読活動には次の2つの目的があると述べています。

（1）音声と文字を結びつけるための音読
（2）語彙や文法規則を内在化させるための音読

　鈴木（2005）が述べているように，音読活動はアウトプット活動ではなく，語彙や文法規則を内在化させることを目的としているので，インテイク活動と位置付けることができます。つまり，音読活動を授業のゴールに設定している授業は，第二言語習得研究における認知プロセスの大きな枠組みである「インプット→インテイク→アウトプット」において，「インプット→インテイク」に留まった指導であり，「アウトプット」を欠いた指導と言えます。このことから，音読を授業のゴールに設定するのは適切な指導ではないと言えるでしょう。

　音読指導には様々な方法がありますが，ここではリテリングにつながりやすい音読法をいくつか紹介します。紹介する音読法をすべて行う必要はなく，生徒の英語習熟度に応じて選択してください。*Compass English CommunicationI Revised*（大修館書店，平成29年度発行）のLESSON 9 The Story of Chocolate のPart1を題材にして解説をします。

Lesson 9  The Story of Chocolate
［Part 1］
　Do you like chocolate? Many people do. Chocolate is very popular in Ja-

pan and in many other countries. Yet how much do you know about chocolate?

The story of chocolate started in the rainforests of Central America. That is the place where people first grew cacao trees. Chocolate is made from the seeds of the cacao tree. (以下省略)

## 3.1　Read aloud, Listen and Repeat

　教師が句・節・文の日本語を言い，生徒はその日本語に該当する句・節・文を音読します。この音読法では，まずは生徒に自力で音読させる機会を与えます。この時点では，間違って音読しても構いません。その後で，教師によるモデルを聞かせ，生徒はそのモデルを正確に模倣します。意味のまとまりで区切るので，意味を意識した音読をさせることができます。

【指導の流れ】　※Ｔは教師　Ｓは生徒
Ｔ：日本語に該当する箇所を音読してください。
　　あなたはチョコレートが好きですか？
Ｓ：Do you like chocolate?
Ｔ：Do you like chocolate?
Ｓ：Do you like chocolate?
Ｔ：好きな人が多いです。
Ｓ：Many people do.
Ｔ：Many people do.
Ｓ：Many people do.
Ｔ：チョコレートはとても人気があります。
Ｓ：Chocolate is very popular
Ｔ：Chocolate is very popular
Ｓ：Chocolate is very popular
Ｔ：日本と多くの他の国々で
Ｓ：in Japan and in many other countries.
Ｔ：in Japan and in many other countries.

S：in Japan and in many other countries.

## 3.2　Overlapping ＋ペン置き音読

　Read aloud, Listen and Repeat で正確に音読できるようになった後に行う音読です。Overlapping では，生徒は教師または CD 音声のモデルを聞き，英文を見ながら音読します。モデルをしっかりと聞きながら，リズムやイントネーションなどを意識して模倣します。また，モデルのスピードに付いていくように指導します。うまくできるようになったら，シャープペンシルやボールペンなどを英文の上に縦や斜めに適当に置いて，部分的に見えなくなった状態で行うと，次に紹介する Shadowing につながる音読となるでしょう。

【指導の流れ】
　　　T：CD 音声を聞き，本文を見ながら CD 音声とほぼ同時に音読してください。リズムやイントネーションも模倣しながら，スピードにも付いていってください。
CD 音声：Do you like chocolate? Many people do.
　　　S： Do you like chocolate? Many people do.
CD 音声：Chocolate is very popular in Japan …
　　　S： Chocolate is very popular in Japan …

## 3.3　Shadowing

　Overlapping が正確にできるようになった後に行う音読です。Overlapping とは異なり，生徒は教師または CD 音声のモデルを聞きながら，英文を見ない状態で音読します。モデルをしっかりと聞きながら，リズムやイントネーションなどを模倣する点は同じです。Overlapping と Shadowing は流暢さを伸長させることができます。

【指導の流れ】
　　　T：CD 音声を聞きながら，本文を見ないで CD 音声とほぼ同時に

音読してください。リズムやイントネーションも模倣しながら，スピードにも付いていってください。

CD 音声：Do you like chocolate? Many people do.

    S ： Do you like chocolate? Many people do.

CD 音声：Chocolate is very popular in Japan …

    S ： Chocolate is very popular in Japan …

## 3.4 Read and Look up

　教師が句・節・文の日本語を言った後で "Read." と指示をします。生徒は "Read." の指示を受けて，その日本語に該当する句・節・文を発声せずに頭の中で繰り返し音読します。数秒後に（頭の中で 2，3 回音読できる時間），教師は "Look up." と指示し，その指示によって生徒は顔を上げ，頭の中で音読した箇所を発声します。この音読では，数秒間，句・節・文を記憶に留めてから発声するので，語彙，文法項目，重要構文を内在化させる効果があります。Read and Look up は英語力の向上に非常に有益な音読法ですので，全文に対して行うのが理想的ですが，時間がかかる上に，生徒が飽きてしまう恐れがあるので，リテリングで使用させたい内容や表現の入った文だけを扱うのがよいでしょう。

**【指導の流れ】**

T：あなたはチョコレートが好きですか？ "Read."

S：（本文中にある Do you like chocolate? を頭の中で繰り返し音読する。）

T：（数秒後）"Look up."

S：（顔を上げて）Do you like chocolate?

T：好きな人が多いです。"Read."

S：（本文中にある Many people do. を頭の中で繰り返し音読する。）

T：（数秒後）"Look up."

S：（顔を上げて）Many people do.

T：チョコレートはとても人気があります。"Read."

S：（本文中にある Chocolate is very popular を頭の中で繰り返し音読する。）

T：（数秒後）"Look up."

S：（顔を上げて）Chocolate is very popular

T：日本と多くの他の国々で "Read."

S：（本文中にある in Japan and in many other countries. を頭の中で繰り返し音読する。）

T：（数秒後）"Look up."

S：（顔を上げて）in Japan and in many other countries.

## 3.5 「日→英」通訳

　意味のまとまりごとに日本語を英語に変換する音読であり，「日→英」通訳用のハンドアウトを作成して使用することが多いです。本文の再生であるリプロダクションができないと，自分の言葉で話すリテリングをするのは難しいので，まずはリプロダクションをできるようにするためにも，この音読法は有益です。

### 【「日→英」通訳用のハンドアウト例】

| 日本語 | 英語 |
|---|---|
| あなたはチョコレートが好きですか？ | Do you like chocolate? |
| 多くの人々は好きです。 | Many people do. |
| チョコレートはとても人気があります<br>日本と多くの他の国々で | Chocolate is very popular<br>in Japan and in many other countries. |
| しかし，<br>あなたはチョコレートについてどのくらい知っていますか | Yet<br>how much do you know about chocolate? |
| チョコレートの物語は始まりました<br>中央アメリカの雨林で | The story of chocolate started<br>in the rainforests of Central America. |
| あれは場所です<br>人々が最初にカカオの木を育てた | That is the place<br>where people first grew cacao trees. |

| | |
|---|---|
| チョコレートは作られる<br>カカオの木の種から | Chocolate is made<br>from the seeds of the cacao tree. |

　左側に意味のまとまりごとに分けられた日本語，右側にその日本語に対応するように英語を記載して，ペアでAが意味のまとまりごとに日本語を言い，Bがそれを英語に変換します。もちろん，ペアでの活動の前には個人による練習が必要です。

## 【指導の流れ】

（以下は，個人練習後のペアによる活動における指導の流れです）

S1：あなたはチョコレートが好きですか？

S2：Do you like chocolate?

S1：多くの人々は好きです。

S2：Many people do.

S1：チョコレートはとても人気があります。

S2：Chocolate is very popular

S1：日本と多くの他の国々で

S2：in Japan and in many other countries.

S1：しかし

S2：Yet

S1：あなたはチョコレートについてどのくらい知っていますか

S2：how much do you know about chocolate?

## 3.6　穴埋め音読

　以下のような本文に空欄を入れたハンドアウトを使用して音読します。リテリングにつながりやすいように，要点に関連するキーワードを空欄にすることもできますし，名詞，動詞，形容詞のような品詞ごとに空欄を作成することもできます。また，文法項目の入った部分を空欄にすることもでき，様々な目的に応じて空欄を作成することができます。

> Do you like （　　　）? Many people do. Chocolate is very （　　　） in Japan and in many （　　　） countries. （　　　） how much do you （　　　） about chocolate?
>
> The story of chocolate （　　　） in the rainforests of Central America. That is the place （　　　） people first （　　　） cacao trees. Chocolate （　　　）（　　　） from the （　　　） of the cacao tree.

## 3.7　なりきり音読

　場面をイメージして，本文の登場人物になりきって音読します。人に意味を伝えることを意識した音読はコミュニケーション能力を育成する観点からも重要であり，本文の解釈において，「誰が」，「誰に対して」，「いつ」，「何を」，「どのように」，「なぜ」伝えようとしているのかを考えさせながら音読させることがポイントとなります。
※「指導の流れ」は省略します。

### 第3章のまとめ

〈リテリングの手順〉
　（Ⅰ）内容理解
　（Ⅱ）**音読による内在化**
　（Ⅲ）発話情報の選定
　（Ⅳ）英語への変換
　（Ⅴ）発話

- ●音読活動には，「音声と文字を結びつけるための音読」と「語彙や文法規則を内在化させるための音読」の2つの目的がある。
- ●「インプット→インテイク→アウトプット」という第二言語習得の大きな枠組みから考えると，音読活動を授業のゴールに設定すべきではない。

●音読指導法①「Read aloud, Listen and Repeat」

　教師が句・節・文の日本語を言い，生徒はその日本語に該当する句・節・文を音読する。次に，生徒はその箇所に対する教師によるモデルを聞き，そのモデルを模倣する。

　［利点］

　　意味のまとまりで区切るので，意味を意識した音読をさせることができる。また，教師によるモデルを提示することで，生徒が自力で音読できるかを確認できる。

●音読指導法②「Overlapping ＋ ペン置き音読」

　生徒は教師または CD 音声のモデルを聞き，英文を見ながら音読する。うまくできるようになったら，シャープペンシルやボールペンなどを英文の上に置いて行う。

　［利点］

　　モデルを聞くことで，リズムやイントネーションなどの音声面を意識した音読をさせることができる。また，流暢さを伸長させることができ，Shadowing のための準備トレーニング音読としての役割も兼ねる。

●音読指導法③「Shadowing」

　生徒は教師または CD 音声のモデルを聞きながら，英文を見ない状態で音読する。

　［利点］

　　Overlapping と同様に，リズムやイントネーションなどの音声面を意識した音読をさせることができる。また，音声を知覚する能力を伸長させ，リスニング力も育成することができる。

●音読指導法④「Read and Look up」

　教師が句・節・文の日本語を言った後で "Read." と指示し，生徒は，その日本語に該当する箇所を発声せずに頭の中で繰り返し音読し，数秒後に顔を上げて発声する。

［利点］

　数秒間，句・節・文を記憶に留めてから発声するので，語彙，文法項目，重要構文を内在化させる効果がある。

●音読指導法⑤「日→英」通訳

「日→英」通訳用のハンドアウトを使用して，意味のまとまりごとに日本語を英語に変換する。

　［利点］

　この音読を行うことで，リプロダクションができるようになる。また，口頭英作文とも呼べる活動なので，ライティング力の育成もできる。

●音読指導法⑥「穴埋め音読」

本文に空欄を入れたハンドアウトを使用して音読する。指導のねらいに応じて，空欄の場所を決めることができる。

　［利点］

　名詞，動詞，形容詞のような品詞ごとに空欄を作成することができるので，特定の語彙や表現の内在化を促すことができる。

●音読指導法⑦「なりきり音読」

場面をイメージして，本文の登場人物になりきって音読する。

　［利点］

　「誰が」，「誰に対して」，「いつ」，「何を」，「どのように」，「なぜ」伝えようとしているのかを考えさせながら音読させることができるので，人に意味を伝える音読になる。

# リテリングの手順（Ⅲ）：発話情報の選定

　本文を理解し，本文の言語材料の内在化のために音読をした後は，本文中のどの情報を発話するのか，つまり，要点だけを発話するのか，細部情報も含めて発話するのかを決めなければなりません。また，生徒の英語習熟度を考慮して，発話部分は単語レベルに留めるのか，1文を発話させるのかなども考慮すべき点でしょう。リテリングをするときには，話したい内容を何も見ずに思い出しながら発話するのは記憶の負荷が高いので，内容を思い出しやすいような手がかりを使用することをお薦めします。

## 4.1　どのくらい発話させるのか

　英語習熟度の低い生徒にとっては，リテリングは負荷の高い活動であるため，上手に発話することができません。このような生徒には，例えば，穴埋めプリントを作成して，単語レベルの再生から始めるのがよいでしょう。その後，「単語レベル → フレーズレベル → 1文レベル → パラグラフレベル」と発話の範囲を拡大していくことができます。以下は，*Revised LANDMARK English Communication I*（啓林館，平成29年度発行）の LESSON 10 Friendship over Time の Part 3 を題材としたプリント作成例です。

Lesson 10  Friendship over Time

［Part 1］

　On March 17th, 1985, during the Iran-Iraq War, Iraq suddenly announced, "Forty-eight hours from now, we will shoot down any airplanes flying over Iran." Foreign people in Iran began to return home in a hurry on the airlines of their home countries. Unfortunately, at that time, there was no regular airline service between Iran and Japan.

The Japanese embassy in Iran made every effort to get seats on foreign airlines. However, they gave top priority to the people of their home countries and refused to accept the Japanese passengers. More than 200 Japanese people were left in Iran. Just when they were losing hope of going home, the Japanese embassy received a phone call: "Turkish airlines will offer special seats for the Japanese people left in Iran." Two planes from Turkey appeared in the sky and helped the Japanese out of Iran. It was one hour and fifteen minutes before the deadline.

The next day the Japanese media took the rescue up as their top news. But they did not know the real reason why Turkey saved the Japanese at the risk of being shot down. The Turkish ambassador to Japan explained later, "One of the reasons is that the Turkish people have good feelings toward the Japanese people. This is because of the Ertugrul accident in 1890." What was the Ertugrul accident? It goes back to the Meiji era in Japan.

[Part 2]

On September 16th, 1890, a strong typhoon hit Oshima Island, Wakayama. Stormy winds began to blow against the Kashinozaki lighthouse, which stood on a steep cliff at the eastern edge of Oshima.

In the evening, a big man rushed into the lighthouse keepers' room. He was all wet, covered with blood, and clearly not Japanese. The keepers soon understood that an accident had happened at sea. "Whose ship are you on? How many crew members do you have?"

".........."

The keepers couldn't make themselves understood in Japanese.

The keepers took out a book which had pictures of national flags. The injured man slowly pointed his finger at the red flag with a white crescent moon and a star in its center.

"This flag ...Turkey!"

With gestures, the Turkish man told them that the ship had sunk and all the crew had been thrown into the sea. He had managed to swim to the beach and climb up the cliff.

The villagers, who heard of the accident from the lighthouse keepers, quickly began to rescue the other crew members. But it was dangerous work in the middle of a typhoon. Some villagers pulled the injured crew members up the cliff by rope. Others climbed up the steep cliff, carrying the large Turkish people on their shoulders. After that, they took their clothes off and, with their bodies, warmed the survivors shivering with cold.

［Part 3］　※指導例として Part 3 を使用します。

> The name of the Turkish ship was "the Ertugrul." It was an old-fashioned wooden warship with 650 crew members. The accident happened on the way from Yokohama to Kobe. There were only 69 survivors. If the villagers had not helped them, all the crew would have lost their lives.
>
> Although the poor villagers did not have enough food for themselves, they offered precious rice and sweet potatoes to the survivors. Even the women and children gave their own clothes to the naked crew members. When they ran out of food, the villagers even gave them the chickens which were kept to tell time.
>
> Although the villagers did not know any Turkish at all, they encouraged the injured survivors in Japanese and took care of them for three days. The Turkish people thanked the villagers with all their hearts and kept the kindness of the villagers in their minds.

［Part 4］

Early on the morning of September 20th, a German warship arrived at Oshima to take the survivors to Kobe. At noon they were seen off by the villagers, who had taken care of them until just a few minutes before.

"Get home safely."

"Good-bye."

All the crew that could walk on their own came onto the deck. They waved good-bye to the villagers until the port was out of sight.

After a month's stay in Kobe, the 69 Turkish survivors left Japan for their home on two Japanese warships on October 11th, 1890. They arrived safely in Turkey on January 2nd, 1891. A lot of Japanese people learned about the accident through the newspapers and sent money to the families of the dead crew members.

Now we understand why the Turkish government decided to rescue the Japanese people during the Iran-Iraq War. The Ertugrul story has been passed on for generations in Turkey and its people keep a strong friendship with the Japanese. The Ertugrul brought Japan and Turkey together. The bridge between the two countries has grown over time.

## 【単語レベルの再生】

The name of the Turkish ship was "the (      ) ." It was an (      ) wooden warship with 650 crew members. The accident happened on the way from (      ) to Kobe. There were only 69 (      ) . If the villagers had not helped them, all the crew would have (      ) their lives.

Although the poor villagers did not have enough (      ) for themselves, they offered precious rice and sweet potatoes to the (      ) . Even the women and children gave their own (      ) to the naked crew members. When they ran out of (      ) , the villagers even gave them the (      ) which were kept to tell time.

Although the villagers did not know any Turkish at all, they (      ) the injured (      ) in Japanese and took care of them for three days. The Turkish people (      ) the villagers with all their hearts and kept the (      ) of the villagers in their minds.

## 【フレーズレベルの再生／産出】

(      ) was "the Ertugrul." It was (      ) with 650 crew members. The accident happened (      ) . There were (      ) . If the villagers had not helped them, all the crew would (      ) .

Although the poor villagers did not have enough food for themselves, they

(　　　　　) to the survivors. Even the women and children (　　　　)
to the naked crew members. When they (　　　　　) , the villagers even
gave them the chickens which were kept (　　　　) .

　　Although the villagers did not know any Turkish at all, they (　　　　)
in Japanese and (　　　　) them for three days. The Turkish people
thanked the villagers with all their hearts and kept the kindness of the villagers
(　　　　) .

【1文レベルの再生 / 産出】

The name　　＿＿＿＿＿＿＿＿＿＿＿＿＿＿＿＿＿＿＿＿＿＿＿＿＿ .
It was　　＿＿＿＿＿＿＿＿＿＿＿＿＿＿＿＿＿＿＿＿＿＿＿＿＿＿＿ .
The accident　　＿＿＿＿＿＿＿＿＿＿＿＿＿＿＿＿＿＿＿＿＿＿＿ .
There　　＿＿＿＿＿＿＿＿＿＿＿＿＿＿＿＿＿＿＿＿＿＿＿＿＿＿＿ .
If the villagers　　＿＿＿＿＿＿＿＿＿＿＿＿＿＿＿＿＿＿＿＿＿＿ .
Although　　＿＿＿＿＿＿＿＿＿＿＿＿＿＿＿＿＿＿＿＿＿＿＿＿＿ .
Even　　＿＿＿＿＿＿＿＿＿＿＿＿＿＿＿＿＿＿＿＿＿＿＿＿＿＿＿ .
When　　＿＿＿＿＿＿＿＿＿＿＿＿＿＿＿＿＿＿＿＿＿＿＿＿＿＿＿ .
Although　　＿＿＿＿＿＿＿＿＿＿＿＿＿＿＿＿＿＿＿＿＿＿＿＿＿ .
The Turkish　　＿＿＿＿＿＿＿＿＿＿＿＿＿＿＿＿＿＿＿＿＿＿＿ .

【パラグラフレベルの再生 / 産出】

パラグラフ1
the Ertugrul / warship / accident / 69 survivors / their lives
パラグラフ2
offered / clothes / chickens / time
パラグラフ3
encouraged / three days / thanked / kindness

## 4.2　どのように手がかりを提示するのか

　　手がかりを使用するときには，教師が選択して提示する方法と生徒に選
択させる方法があります。教師が選択する場合には，英語習熟度に応じて，
重要度を考慮して手がかりを選択することができます。一方，生徒が選択

する場合には，自分の能力に応じて手がかりを選択できるだけでなく，自己決定の要素が加わることで，リテリングへの動機が高まり，より主体的な活動になる可能性が高くなります。しかし，生徒が選択する場合には，特に英語習熟度の低い生徒は手がかりを必要以上に多く選択する傾向があるので，教師は手がかりの数を制限するのがよいでしょう。

　手がかりが必要となるのは，フレーズレベル以上のリテリングを行う場合です。英語習熟度の低い生徒にも配慮し，記憶の負荷を下げる目的で内容を思い出しやすいような手がかりを使用します。手がかりの使用には，以下の3つの方法があります。

（1）キーワードと絵や写真の両方を使用する。
　　　［英語習熟度が低い生徒用］
（2）キーワードだけを使用する。
　　　［英語習熟度が中程度の生徒用］
（3）絵や写真だけを使用し，キーワードを使用しない。
　　　［英語習熟度が高い生徒用］

　キーワードは英語で記載することもできますし，日本語で記載することもできます。以下に *CROWN English Communication I New Edition*（三省堂，平成29年度発行）の LESSON 1 When Words Won't Work と *Revised LAND-MARK English Communication I*（啓林館，平成29年度発行）の LESSON 10 Friendship over Time における手がかりの例を示します。

LESSON 1 When Words Won't Work

　Words are words and pictures are pictures. Most of our information comes from words. But we are getting more and more information from little pictures. We call them "pictograms."

[Part 1]

　Language is an important means of communication. You exchange greetings. At school you listen to your teachers, have discussions, and enjoy talking with your classmates. At home you do your homework. For all of these activities you use language.

Yet, there is another important means of communication. Look around carefully, and you will notice lots of pictograms. Take a look at the following. Even little kids may know them.

The one on the left shows an emergency exit. The one in the middle shows a restroom. The one on the right shows an escalator.


[Part 2]

Pictograms are often used in public places. Why do people use pictograms instead of words such as "emergency exit," "restroom," or "escalator"? Aren't words better than pictograms?

Pictograms are used for at least two reasons. First, you can usually guess their meanings just by looking at them. However, you cannot understand words if you don't know the language. For this reason, pictograms are used at international airports.

Second, you can quickly recognize pictograms even if they are far away because of their simple design and bright colors. For this reason, they are used on roads.

Take a look at these road signs:

These are not used in Japan, but you can easily guess their meanings: "Drawbridge ahead," "Watch out for kangaroos," and "Roundabout ahead."


[Part 3]

People from different cultures can usually understand pictograms easily. But sometimes they find pictograms confusing. Look at this pictogram:

It tells different people different things. Maybe this man is clearing a landslide. Maybe he is opening an umbrella on a windy day. Actually, this man is working on a road. This is a pictogram for "Roadwork ahead."

You can usually get the message from a pictogram as soon as you see it. But sometimes you have to learn the meaning of a pictogram, just like you learn the words of a foreign language.

Pictograms may never take the place of words, but they are already an important means of communication. Some people are making full sentences and even telling stories with pictograms. A famous Chinese artist wrote the following "sentence." Can you read it?

Will pictograms eventually take the place of words? Will they be the language of the future? What do you think?

## （1）キーワードと絵や写真の両方を使用する

絵については，教師や生徒が以下のイラストのような絵を描いて使用することができます。また，教科書に付属するイラストデータがある場合は，出版社から使用許可が取れた場合に使用することができます。

LESSON 1 When Words Won't Work

discussion                    lots of pictograms

simple design

tell different people
different things

Will pictograms eventually
take the place of words?

## （2）英語によるキーワードだけを使用する

LESSON 10  Friendship over Time（※本文は 4.1 を参照）

［Part 1］

Forty-eight hours / regular airline service / Japanese embassy / top priority / 200 Japanese people / phone call / special seats / deadline / top news / real reason / good feelings / Ertugrul accident

［Part 2］

September 16th, 1890 / strong typhoon / steep cliff / lighthouse keeper's room / crew members / book / white crescent moon / gestures / rescue / rope / shoulders / clothes

[Part 3]

old-fashioned wooden / 650 / Yokohama / 69 / precious rice / naked / chickens / in Japanese / three days / kindness

[Part 4]

September 20th / German warship / good-bye / October 11th,1890 / January 2nd, 1891 / money / Ertugrul story / strong friendship

## （3）日本語によるキーワードだけを使用する

LESSON 10  Friendship over Time

[Part 1]

48 時間 / 定期便 / 日本大使館 / 最優先 / 200 人の日本人 / 電話 / 特別席 / 最終期限 / トップニュース / 本当の理由 / よい感情 / エルトゥールル号の事故

[Part 2]

1890 年 9 月 16 日 / 強い台風 / 険しい崖 / 灯台守の部屋 / 乗組員 / 本 / 白い三日月 / 身ぶり / 救助する / ロープ / 肩 / 服

[Part 3]

旧式の木造軍艦 / 650 名 / 横浜 / 69 名 / 貴重なお米 / 裸の / ニワトリ / 日本語で / 3 日間 / 親切

[Part 4]

9 月 20 日 / ドイツの軍艦 / さようなら / 1890 年 10 月 11 日 / 1891 年 1 月 2 日 / お金 / エルトゥールル号の話 / 強い友情

（4）絵や写真だけを使用し，キーワードを使用しない

LESSON 10  Friendship over Time

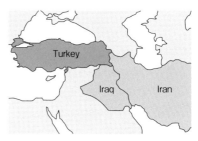

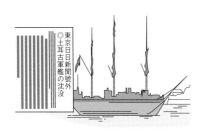

　以下は，*CROWN English Communication I New Edition*（三省堂，平成29年度発行）の LESSON 3  A Canoe Is an Island を題材として，生徒が作成したリテリング用の手がかりメモです。

Lesson 3  A Canoe Is an Island

In 2007, the Hawaiian canoe Hōkūleʻa and another boat Kama Hele sailed from Hawaii all the way to Japan. Uchino Kanako was a crew member. Here's her story.

[Part 1]

I have always loved the sea. When I was in college, I visited Miyake-jima with a friend of mine. I explored the ocean and fell in love with its beauty. Ever since this visit, I have really been interested in the sea.

I knew I had to learn more about the sea, but I didn't know where I could study. And then I found a book about Nainoa Thompson and the Hōkūleʻa. I read about how this native Hawaiian learned traditional navigation skills from his master Mau Piailug of Satawal. I also learned that the Hōkūleʻa successfully sailed from Hawaii to Tahiti in 1976 by using traditional navigation.

I became very interested in the ancient skills needed to navigate across the ocean. I made up my mind to go to Hawaii, and to take a look at the Hōkūleʻa with my own eyes.

[Part 2]

After I finished college, I went to Hawaii to study ocean ecology at the University of Hawaii.

I went to see the Hōkūleʻa. She was back from a long voyage. I began to participate in repairing the Hōkūleʻa for the next voyage. I trained to be part of the crew. I learned about traditional navigation and Hawaiian culture.

In 2007, the Hōkūleʻa was planning a five-month voyage from Hawaii to Micronesia, and then to Japan. I felt honored when I was asked to be a crew member on the canoe from Micronesia to Japan.

In January 2007, the Hōkūleʻa started out. On the 56th day, we arrived at Satawal in Micronesia. People welcomed us warmly. They carried a sign saying, "Welcome to Satawal."

Then we headed for Okinawa. We were able to see the Big Dipper. We could also see the Southern Cross. Being familiar with the movement of about 220 stars was just one of the skills which we needed. We also learned to read the movement of the waves and changes in wind direction. We were on our way to Okinawa, slowly but steadily.

[Part 3]

The crew members who were on the Hōkule'a were busy. The most important job was steering the canoe. Three teams took turns. My team worked from 10 a.m. to 2 p.m., and then from 10 p.m. to 2 a.m. The team steering the canoe had to stay alert all the time.

One night, the ocean was exceptionally calm. The sea was so quiet that you could even see the reflection of the stars. I was the only one on deck, and I felt very peaceful. I also felt very much connected to the great universe. I was one tiny person on a tiny canoe. But the fact is that I was part of the whole.

After leaving Micronesia, we traveled a distance of almost 2,000 kilometers. The stars and the sun and the waves guided us. As we got near Okinawa, I felt that we were one big family.

It was morning. "Look! I can see something," cried one of the crew members. It was an island—Okinawa. But to me at that moment, it was much more than an island. Land, water, people and other life in the middle of this vast ocean. It was truly a miracle.

[Part 4]

On June 9, 2007, we reached Yokohama, the end of our trip. As I think about the voyage, I have a deeper appreciation for our relationship with nature.

Traditional navigation teaches us how to see nature. It also teaches us that nature is providing everything we need. We have to learn how nature works in order to receive its gifts.

The Hawaiians say: "A canoe is an island, and an island is a canoe." We can also think of our planet Earth as a canoe in the vast universe. What are we doing with "our canoe"? What do we value? Where do we want to go? What is our role as crew members on our canoe? After the voyage to Japan, the Hōkūle'a set sail to go around the world in 2014 to raise these questions.

We are all part of nature. We can learn to work together with nature to make our canoe, our earth, a more beautiful and harmonious place for all life.

　　以下に挙げる生徒が作成したこのリテリング用の手がかりメモでは，生徒は本文を読みながら，本文内容の要約を目的として，Part ごとにメモを作成しました。英語をたくさん使用するより，イラストや矢印などの記号をできるだけ多く使用することで視覚的にも理解しやすく，まとまりのあるメモに仕上がっています。

〈生徒作品 A〉

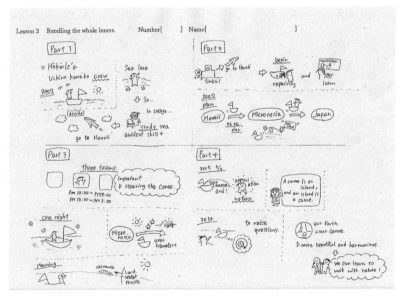

〈生徒作品 B〉

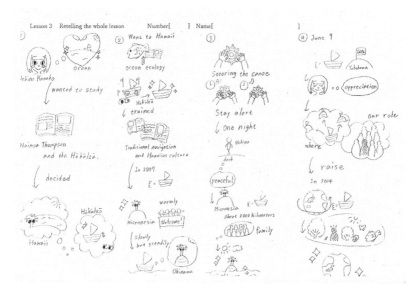

　さらに，ここで，「意味順」BOX を使用して手がかりを記載する方法を紹介します。「意味順」とは，京都大学の田地野彰名誉教授（現　名古屋外国語大学教授）が考案された学習法・指導法です（田地野（2011）など）。「意味順」では，英語の大きな言語的特徴の１つである「語順」に注目し，「だれが」，「する（です）」，「だれ・なに」，「どこ」，「いつ」を基本とした英語の文における意味のまとまりごとに従って語（句）を並べるだけで正しい英文が作れるシステムです。例えば，「昨日，警察は家の中で盗まれた指輪を発見した。」という日本文を「意味順」BOX に当てはめると表4-1 のようになります。

| だれが | する（です） | だれ・なに | どこ | いつ |
|---|---|---|---|---|
| 警察は | 見つけた | 盗まれた | 家の中で | 昨日 |
| The police | found | the stolen ring | in the house | yesterday |

表4-1　「意味順」BOX の例

また「意味順」では，「文の組み立て方」を「横軸」（意味順）として位置付け，その構成要素を「縦軸」（文法項目）として関連付けることができます。例えば，「だれが」BOX に入るのは，名詞，代名詞，冠詞であり，「する（です）」BOX に入るのは，進行形，完了形，助動詞，受動態，仮定法などといったように，横軸と縦軸の二次元でとらえることができるのです。「意味順」を使用することで，語順の間違いがなくなる，主語を付け忘れなくなる，そのまま直訳しなくなるといった効果が確認されています。この「意味順」BOX をリテリングで使用するときには，本文を読んで，手がかりを「意味順」BOX の中に記載します。表4-2, 4-3 に使用例を示します。

　また，教師が手がかりを選択する場合には，パラフレーズをした語句を「意味順」BOX 内に置くことで生徒のパラフレーズを促すこともできるでしょう。

| だれが | する（です） | だれ・なに | どこ | いつ |
|---|---|---|---|---|
| ピクトグラム | 使われる |  | 公共の場所 |  |
| あなた | 推測できる | その意味 |  |  |
| あなた | 認識できる | ピクトグラム |  |  |
| ピクトグラム | 使われている |  | 道路 |  |

表4-2　日本語による手がかり例

| だれが | する（です） | だれ・なに | どこ | いつ |
|---|---|---|---|---|
| pictograms | are used |  | public places |  |
| you | can guess | the meanings |  |  |
| you | can recognize | pictograms |  |  |
| pictograms | are used |  | on roads |  |

表4-3　英語による手がかり例

## 4.3　どのように手がかりを選ぶのか

　手がかりを使用するときには，話す内容が本文中において，重要度が高い「要点」であるのか，あるいは，重要度が低い「細部情報」であるのかを判断した上で選択するのがよいでしょう。以下のように重要度に応じて，3つの方法に分類することができます。

（1）要点に関連した手がかりだけを選択する。
　　　［英語習熟度が低い生徒用］
（2）細部情報に関連した手がかりだけを選択する。
　　　［英語習熟度が高い生徒用］
（3）要点と細部情報に関連した手がかりを両方とも選択する。
　　　［英語習熟度が中程度の生徒用］

　以下は *Genius English Communication I Revised*（大修館書店，平成29年度発行）の LESSON 8 Water Crisis の Part 1 を題材にして，重要度の異なる手がかりを示しています。＿＿＿は要点に関連した手がかりであり，＿＿＿は細部情報に関連した手がかりを示します。これはあくまで一例ですので，生徒の習熟度に応じて，どの手がかりを選択するのがよいか，選択数をどうするのかを判断してください。

LESSON 8　Water Crisis
［Part 1］
　The Earth is often called "The Water Planet." Over 70 percent of its surface is covered with water. Almost all of the water, however, is seawater and only 0.01 percent of it is good for drinking. About 900,000,000 people, one eighth of the world population, have no safe water to drink. If there were no safe water at all, we could not live.
　The World Wide Fund for Nature (WWF) says that water shortages are a problem even in the most developed countries. Economic wealth does not al-

ways mean a lot of water. Some of the world's wealthiest cities such as Houston and Sydney are using more water than they can supply. In London, leaks from aging water pipes are wasting 300 Olympic swimming pools' worth of water every single day. At the same time, southern Europe is becoming drier as a result of climate change, while further north Alpine glaciers ― an important source of water ― are shrinking.

To make matters worse, a rapid increase in the world population and global water shortages seem almost certain to happen. The WWF calls for water conservation on a global scale and asks rich states to set an example by improving water supply systems and solving climate problems.

## 4.4 どのタイミングで手がかりを提示するのか

手がかりを提示するタイミングとしては，例えば，ペアによるリテリングの場合には，以下のように３つに分類できます。

（1）個人練習後のペアによるリテリングの直前に提示する。
（2）ペアによるリテリングの前に行う個人練習の前に提示する。
（3）内容理解の前に提示する。

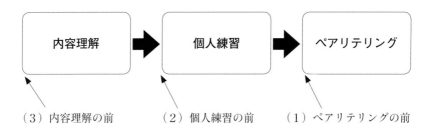

個人練習の段階で手がかりを提示して練習をさせると，次に行うペアによるリテリングでは，本文の言語材料と同じかほぼ同じ英語が発話され，リプロダクションになる可能性が高くなります。一方，手がかりを提示せずに，個人練習をさせ，ペアによるリテリングの直前に提示する場合には，

個人練習の直前に提示する場合と比較して，より即興性が高まるので，パラフレーズされた英語がより多く発話される可能性が高くなります。さらに，難易度が上がりますが，本文の内容理解前に手がかり（キーワードと絵や写真の両方を使用するのが好ましい）を提示することで，本文の内容を自由に推測しながら話す即興型のアウトプット活動を行うこともできます。内容理解の前に行うことで，内容理解への動機を高める効果も期待できます。著者は，これを「推測リテリング」と名付けています。

　以下は，*CROWN English Communication I New Edition*（三省堂，平成29年度発行）のLESSON 6 Roots & Shoots を題材として，手がかりとして本文に関連するキーワードとイラストを見せ，日本語による推測リテリングをさせた後に，英語による推測リテリングをさせ，それをICレコーダーに録音して，書き起こした1人の生徒の発話データです。

　ジェーン・グドールは，Dolittle からチンパンジーを知った。チンパンジー，あっ，ジェーン・グドールはチンパンジーについて興味を持った。それから彼女は，チンパンジーを観察したいと思った。チンパンジーと人は多くの共通点を持つ。例えば，DNA や行動，脳など。また，彼らは集団を作る。そこでは，縄張りをパトロールしたり，お互いを助け合ったり，また，彼らは親切で，愛情深い。

　Jane Goodall knew chimpanzee from Dolittle. She interested in chimpanzee. And then, she want to observe chimpanzee. Someday, chimpanzee and human being have a lot in common. For example, DNA. Behavior, and brain. They makes community. They patrol territory. They are kind and loving. They patrol territories and help one another. They also… They are also kind and loving.


　「推測リテリング」では，まず，数分，時間を与えて，手がかりを見ながら，自由に本文の内容を推測させます。その後，日本語によるリテリングをさせます。ペアやグループの形態で行うと，オリジナルの内容のリテリングを聞くことができ，非常に楽しい活動となるでしょう。特に，物語文の場合は，自由さが増し，予想もつかないようなユニークなストーリーも現れ，笑いが沸き起こるでしょう。次に，日本語で話した内容について，英語で表現するのですが，基本的には準備時間は与えず，手がかりは日本語によるリテリングと同じものを使用します。準備時間を与えないので，即興的なスピーキング活動となります。生徒の英語習熟度が低い場合には，準備時間を与えてもよいでしょう。

　日本語によるリテリングと英語によるリテリングは両方とも，文字に書き起こすと，それらを比較することができるので，「この日本語に対して，英語ではこう言うこともできたなぁ」といった振り返りをさせることができ，英語による表現の幅を増やすことができます。また，素晴らしい推測

リテリングはクラス内で共有するのもよいでしょう。

## LESSON 6 Roots & Shoots

　Jane Goodall is famous for her work with chimpanzees. Here, Kenji interviews her about her life and work.

[Part 1]

Kenji：Dr. Goodall, thank you so much for taking time for this interview. I know that you spent many years studying chimpanzees in Africa. When did you first decide to go to Africa?

Jane　：It was after I had read the Doctor Dolittle and the Tarzan books. When I was 11, I knew that somehow I would go to Africa to live with animals, study them, and write books about them.

Kenji：I'm sure there are lots of young people who want to work with animals someday. How can they prepare themselves?

Jane　：There are a lot of things you can do in order to understand animals. It is very important that you watch them and observe their behavior. It is also important that you write notes and ask questions. If you are really determined, you will find a way.

[Part 2]

Kenji：You did a lot of fieldwork, observing chimpanzees in the wild. Are they in any way like human beings?

Jane　：Chimpanzees and humans have a lot in common. We know today that the DNA of humans and chimps differs by just a little over one percent. Their brains are very much like ours and much of their behavior is like ours. Like us, they also have much to learn in their childhood. The members of a chimp family are very close, often helping one another. They can feel sad, happy, afraid, and angry.

Kenji：What about their character—I mean, are they friendly? Are they cruel?

Jane ： They are usually friendly with each other, but they can be cruel, just like humans.

Kenji ： Really?

Jane ： The males patrol their territories, sometimes attacking chimps from another community. But they can be very kind and loving too. Once, when he was about three years old, a chimp called Mel lost his mother and was left alone. We all thought he'd die. But, to our surprise, a 12-year-old male chimp called Spindle took care of him.

Kenji ： In what way?

Jane ： He let Mel ride on his back and share his nest at night. I often saw him sharing his food if Mel asked for it. Chimpanzees can indeed be loving and caring.

[Part 3]

Kenji ： Now let's turn to the topic of the environment. You travel all over the world, giving talks about the conservation of nature. Do you have any comment?

Jane ： Yes, we humans must understand that wild animals have the right to live. They need wild places. Besides, for our own good, there are some kinds of living things that we must not destroy. Many drugs for human diseases come from plants and insects. When we destroy a wild area, maybe we are destroying the cure for cancer and other diseases without knowing it.

Kenji ： I see.

Jane ： Everything in nature is connected. Plants and animals make up a whole pattern of life. If we destroy that pattern, all kinds of things can go wrong.

Kenji ： Could you say more about that?

Jane ： Sure. One time in England, rabbits were destroying farmers' grain.

The farmers killed the rabbits by giving them a disease. Then foxes didn't have enough to eat and they started killing the farmers' chickens. The farmers then killed the foxes, and rats quickly increased in number and destroyed just as much grain as the rabbits had eaten. We humans are in danger of destroying our environment and ourselves along with it.

［Part 4］

Kenji：So, are you worried about our future?

Jane ：Yes, I am. But my hope lies in young people. Once they know about environmental problems, they want to solve them. That's why I decided to start Roots & Shoots.

Kenji：What's that?

Jane ：Well, it began with a group of high school students in Tanzania in 1991. It is called Roots & Shoots, because roots can work their way through rocks to reach water. And shoots, though they are tiny, can break through a wall to reach the sunlight. The rocks and wall are the problems humans have caused to our earth.

Kenji：So it's a kind of club for young people?

Jane ：That's right. We now have groups all over the world and each group chooses three projects: one to help people, one to help animals, one to help the environment. The world is a better place when you cause a sad person to smile, when you make a dog wag its tail, or when you give water to a thirsty plant. That's what Roots & Shoots is all about.

Kenji：Some final words?

Jane ：The most important difference between humans and chimpanzees is that we can speak and share ideas. Every one of you has a role to play and you can make a difference. You are just one person, but what you do affects the whole world. And you have a choice: What to buy? What to eat? What to wear? The changes you make may be small, but if a thousand, then a million, finally a billion people all make those changes, this is going to make a big change.

Kenji：Dr. Goodall, thank you very much for your time and for sharing your ideas with us.

## 4.5　どのように手がかりを変化させるのか

　手がかりを使用する場合には，1回目のリテリングと2回目以降のリテリングで同じ手がかりを使用する方法と1回目のリテリングと2回目以降のリテリングで異なる手がかりを使用したり，手がかりの数を減らしていく方法があります。

（1）1回目と2回目以降で同じ手がかりを使用する。
　　　［英語習熟度が低い生徒用］
（2）1回目と2回目以降で異なる手がかりを使用する。
　　　［英語習熟度が中程度，高い生徒用］
（3）1回目と2回目以降で手がかりの数を減らす。
　　　［英語習熟度が中程度，高い生徒用］

　Swain（2005）のアウトプット仮説における「気づき機能」とは，アウトプットしたい意味内容を目標言語で表現できないことに気づくことを意味します。1回目と2回目以降で同じ手がかりを使用するリテリングにおける「気づき機能」について考えると，2回目のリテリングの準備段階で，1回目に表現できなかった部分について，もう一度，内容確認と音読をさせることで，「アウトプットの穴」に対して，その穴を埋めさせることができます。英語習熟度の低い生徒にとっては，リテリングは負荷が高い活動です。同じ手がかりを使用させ，何度も練習させることで「穴」をなくし，自信を持ってリテリングを行わせることが大切です。
　1回目と2回目以降で異なる手がかりを使用する利点としては，例えば，1回目の手がかりは要点を中心とした重要度の高い情報を提示し，2回目の手がかりでは年号などの細部情報を提示することで，1回目は，重要度

の高い内容について発話させ，2回目は，それに加えて細部情報についても発話させることができます。また，1回目はキーワードを用いて，2回目は絵だけを用いるなどのバリエーションを取り入れることで，飽きさせない活動にもなります。

　リテリングを数回行う場合には，回数ごとに手がかりを塗りつぶしたり，消しゴムで消して数を減らしたりして，徐々に負荷を上げていく工夫も考えられます。また，即時的なリテリングをさせるならば，他の生徒が選択した手がかりを用いてリテリングをさせても楽しい活動となるでしょう。

## 4.6　どのように家庭学習をさせるのか

　「キーワードと絵や写真の両方を使用する」，「キーワードだけを使用する」，「絵や写真だけを使用し，キーワードを使用しない」といった異なる種類の手がかりを記載したプリントや，同じパートにおいて異なるキーワードを記載した数種類のプリントを配付して，それらを使用して家庭学習としてリテリングを行わせます。また，リテリングの動機を高める工夫として，以下のようなリテリング回数のチェック欄をプリントに記載し，リテリングの回数ごとに数字の書かれた欄を塗りつぶさせます。

| Start | 1 | 2 | 3 | 4 | 5 | 6 | 7 | 8 | Goal |
|---|---|---|---|---|---|---|---|---|---|

## 第4章のまとめ

〈リテリングの手順〉
- （Ⅰ）内容理解
- （Ⅱ）音読による内在化
- （Ⅲ）**発話情報の選定**
- （Ⅳ）英語への変換
- （Ⅴ）発話

- ●発話情報については，「要点だけを発話させる」，「要点に細部情報を加えて発話させる」という2つの種類がある。
- ●発話の範囲には，「単語レベル」，「フレーズレベル」，「1文レベル」，「パラグラフレベル」があり，生徒の英語習熟度によって使い分けるのがよい。
- ●手がかりを提示するときには，教師が手がかりを選択する方法と生徒に手がかりを選択させる方法がある。教師が選択する場合には，手がかりの重要度や生徒の習熟度を考慮できる利点がある。生徒が選択する場合には，自分で選択をしたという自己決定の気持ちが高まり，主体的なリテリングにつながりやすくなる。
- ●手がかりを使用するときには，「キーワードと絵や写真の両方を使用する」，「キーワードだけを使用する」，「絵や写真だけを使用し，キーワードを使用しない」という3つの種類があり，生徒の英語習熟度に応じて使い分けるのがよい。
- ●手がかりの提示においては，「意味順」BOXを使用することもできる。「意味順」BOXを使用してリテリングをさせることで，語順の誤りを減らすことができる。
- ●手がかりを選択するときには，「要点に関連した手がかりだけを選択する」，「細部情報に関連した手がかりだけを選択する」，「要点と細部情報に関連した手がかりを両方とも選択する」という3つの種類があり，生徒の英語習熟度に応じて使い分けるのがよい。

●手がかりを提示するタイミングとして，「個人練習後のペアによる
リテリングの直前に提示する」，「ペアによるリテリングの前に行う
個人練習の前に提示する」，「内容理解の前に提示する」という3つ
の種類がある。「個人練習後のペアによるリテリングの直前に提示
する」では，即興的なリテリングになる可能性が高くなる。「ペア
によるリテリングの前に行う個人練習の前に提示する」では，リプ
ロダクションを強化できる。「内容理解の前に提示する」では，即
興型のアウトプットをさせることができるだけでなく，内容理解へ
の動機付けとなる。

●手がかりを使用する場合には，「1回目と2回目以降で同じ手がか
りを使用する」，「1回目と2回目以降で異なる手がかりを使用す
る」，「1回目と2回目以降で手がかりの数を減らす」という3つの
種類の手がかりの変化があり，生徒の英語習熟度に応じて使い分け
るのがよい。

## 第5章

# リテリングの手順（Ⅳ）：
# 英語への変換

　発話する情報を選定し，発話するための手がかりが整ったら，次は，その情報を英語に変換する段階になりますが，実際には発話される英語の質は以下の3種類に分類できます。

（1）テキストの原文と同じかほぼ同じ＝**リプロダクション**
　　　［英語習熟度が低い生徒］
（2）数ヵ所だけをパラフレーズしたもの
　　　［英語習熟度が中程度の生徒］　　　　　　　　　　リテリング
（3）多くの箇所をパラフレーズしたもの
　　　［英語習熟度が高い生徒］

　以下に，*Revised LANDMARK English Communication I*（啓林館，平成29年度発行）の LESSON 10　Friendship over Time の Part 1 を題材として，それぞれの発話の質の例を示します。

### （1）テキストの原文と同じかほぼ同じ
※以下は本文とほぼ同じ英文

---

　On March 17th, 1985, during the Iran-Iraq War, Iraq announced, "Forty-eight hours from now, we will shoot down any airplanes flying over Iran." Foreign people in Iran began to return home on the airlines of their home countries. At that time, there was no regular airline service between Iran and Japan.

　The Japanese embassy in Iran made every effort to get seats on foreign airlines. But, they gave top priority to the people of their home countries and

---

refused to accept the Japanese passengers. More than 200 Japanese people were left in Iran. When they were losing hope of going home, the Japanese embassy received a phone call: "Turkish airlines will offer special seats for the Japanese people left in Iran." Two planes from Turkey appeared in the sky and helped the Japanese out of Iran. It was one hour and fifteen minutes before the deadline.

## （2）数ヵ所だけをパラフレーズしたもの
※下線部はパラフレーズをした箇所

On March 17th, 1985, during the Iran-Iraq War, Iraq suddenly announced, "Forty-eight hours from now, we will shoot down any airplanes <u>which are flying</u> over Iran." Foreign people in Iran began to <u>go back</u> home in a hurry on the airlines of their home countries. Unfortunately, at that time, there was no regular airline service between Iran and Japan.

The Japanese embassy in Iran made every effort to <u>find</u> seats on foreign airlines. However, they gave top priority to the people of their home countries and <u>did not want</u> to accept the Japanese passengers. More than 200 Japanese people were left in Iran. Just when they were losing hope of going home, the Japanese embassy <u>got</u> a phone call: "Turkish airlines will offer special seats for the Japanese people <u>who were</u> left in Iran." Two planes from Turkey appeared in the sky and helped the Japanese out of Iran. It was one hour and fifteen minutes before the deadline.

## （3）多くの箇所をパラフレーズしたもの
※下線部はパラフレーズをした箇所

On March 17th, 1985, during the Iran-Iraq War, Iraq suddenly announced, "Forty-eight hours from now, <u>all airplanes that fly over Iran will be shot down</u>." <u>People from other countries in Iran started to go back home quickly on their countries' airlines</u>. <u>But</u> at that time there were no <u>airlines flying regularly</u> between Iran and Japan.

<u>The embassy of Japan in Iran tried very hard to find seats on other countries' airlines.</u> But these airlines gave top priority to the people of their <u>own</u> countries and <u>did not want to accept passengers who were Japanese</u>. More than 200 Japanese people <u>had to stay</u> in Iran. Just when <u>these people were giving up hope of going back to Japan, the</u> Japanese embassy <u>got</u> a phone call: "Turkish airlines

will <u>give</u> special seats <u>to</u> the Japanese people <u>who have been left</u> in Iran." Two <u>Turkish</u> planes <u>came out of the sky</u> and <u>helped the Japanese people to leave Iran</u>. <u>That</u> was one hour and fifteen minutes before the deadline <u>given by Iraq</u>.

　リプロダクションは再生活動なので，リプロダクションの指導については，まずは，日本語訳を英語に変換でき，本文の中で出てくる語彙や表現を再生できるようにすることが重要です。基本的な指導としては，「日→英」通訳用のハンドアウトを使用するのがよいでしょう（3.5 を参照）。

　一方，リテリングは再生と産出活動の中間的な位置付けなので再生を求めながらも，これまでに学習した言語知識を総動員して，本文にある語彙や表現を言い換える，つまりパラフレーズすることが必要となります。パラフレーズをすることは，これまでの既習の言語知識を復習することにもなり，またそれらが定着しているかを確認することができます。

　リテリングを目指す指導として，リテリングの後に同じ本文を用いて，どうパラフレーズをすることができたのかを生徒に考えさせるのは有益です。5.1〜5.5 では，*LANDMARK English Communication I*（啓林館，平成25 年度発行）の LESSON 6　The Doctor with the Hands of God を用いたパラフレーズ指導を紹介します。以下，当該レッスンの原文を掲載します。

LESSON 6　The Doctor with the Hands of God
［Part 1］

　Doctor Takanori Fukushima is a Japanese neurosurgeon who works in the United States. He is known as "the man with the Hands of God." People also call him "the Samurai Doctor," "Black Jack," and "the Last Hope." Why do they call him these names?

　By 2007, Dr. Fukushima had operated on more than 20,000 patients around the world. Most of these patients had serious brain tumors that other doctors hesitated to touch. It is amazing that he has been almost 100 percent successful in such difficult operations. He does over 600 operations a year all over the world, and more than 500 patients are still waiting for his help.

These facts tell us how great he is.

[Part 2]

"Everything for the good of the patients" is Dr. Fukushima's motto. In order to do better operations, he invented the "keyhole" method. In traditional brain operations, doctors cut open a large area of the patient's skull, and that brings serious risk to the patient. The "keyhole" method reduces such risk and makes operations much more successful. The method requires only a small hole, about the size of a one-yen coin, on the patient's head. Through this "keyhole" and with the help of a surgical microscope, he can reach the tumor in the patient's brain.

Dr. Fukushima's motto goes beyond his operations. For example, before one operation, a young doctor shaved a female patient's head. As soon as Dr. Fukushima saw some cuts on the patient's head, he said to the doctor, "What on earth have you done to the patient? Look at this poor woman! After the operation, she will look into a mirror and feel sad to find so many cuts on her head. You must consider EVERYTHING for the good of the patient!"

[Part 3]

Dr. Fukushima was born to a priest of the Meiji Shrine in 1942. He was very bright in elementary school, but he was very naughty as well. Once during the winter, for example, he took the chimney pipe from the coal stove and set up a clever trap. When his teacher opened the door of the classroom, the chimney pipe fell and black soot covered her. He was forced to change schools in the third year because of such bad behavior.

During his junior high school years, Dr. Fukushima did not think about his future very seriously. When he was in high school, his favorite uncle, a respected doctor, advised him to become a doctor and help sick people. Dr. Fukushima decided to follow his advice and began to study hard.

A few years later, he got into the School of Medicine at the University of

Tokyo, and entered the field of neurosurgery. There, he met his mentor, Professor Keiji Sano. Dr. Fukushima says, "Professor Sano has a wide knowledge of various sciences and arts as well as medicine. Moreover, he loves his students and cares about them very much. I have always hoped to become like him."

[Part 4]

Today, as an experienced surgeon, Dr. Fukushima teaches his methods to students and younger doctors. One time, during an operation, a younger doctor made a mistake. As soon as Dr. Fukushima noticed it, he took the surgical knife away from the doctor. He then went on lecturing the doctor for six hours while he was correcting the mistake. When he sees younger doctors working too slowly, he always teaches them to work more quickly and carefully. He is a strict teacher but the younger doctors respect him very much. They know that the patient is always his top priority.

Dr. Fukushima is very gentle and friendly with his patients. Even before difficult operations, he always says to them, "I am here for you, so relax. You are in good hands." He does not mean to show off his skills. He only wants all of his patients to feel at peace. He says, "When I see my patients smile after successful operations, I feel truly happy. I believe I have found my purpose in life."

## 5.1 本文の語彙や表現を言い換えよう

　本文中の語彙や表現の言い換えでは，生徒にどのように言い換えることができるのかを考えさせてから，言い換え例を提示します。以下は語彙や表現の言い換え例です。

〈言い換え例〉
Part 1
is known as → is famous as

more than → over

serious → bad

hesitated to → didn't wanted to

amazing → surprising

difficult → hard

all over the world → around the world

Part 2

In order to → To

traditional → conventional

requires → needs

reach → get to

For example → For instance

As soon as → The moment

on earth → in the world

consider → think about

Part 3

bright → cheerful

fell → dropped

was forced to → was made to

follow → take

got into → entered

entered → chose

various → several different

Moreover → In addition

hoped → wanted

Part 4

experienced → veteran

One time → One day

noticed → found

went on lecturing → kept on lecturing

in good hands → safe

feel at peace → feel peaceful

truly → very

## 5.2 文の構造を言い換えよう

　文の構造を言い換える指導は，文法指導にもなります。既習の文法項目を使用することで，文法項目の復習や定着にもなります。以下は文の構造を言い換えた例です。

Part 1

People also call him "the Samurai Doctor,"

→ He is also called "the Samurai Doctor,"

Most of these patients had serious brain tumors that other doctors hesitated to touch.

→ Most of these patients had serious brain tumors. Other doctors hesitated to touch them.

These facts tell us how great he is.

→ From these facts we can know that he is great.

Part 2

and that brings serious risk to the patient

→ and that exposes the patient to serious risk

only a small hole, about the size of a one-yen coin

→ only a small hole which is about the size of a one-yen coin

## Part 3

Dr. Fukushima was born to a priest of the Meiji Shrine in 1942.

→ Dr. Fukushima was born in 1942. His father was a priest of the Meiji Shrine.

he was very naughty as well

→ he was also very playful

black soot covered her

→ she was covered with black soot

in the third year

→ when he was in the third year

because of such bad behavior

→ because he had acted badly

During his junior high school years

→ When he was in junior high school

Professor Sano has a wide knowledge of various sciences and arts

→ Professor Sano knows a lot about various sciences and arts

Part 4

During an operation → When he was doing an operation

his top priority → the most important thing

I am here for you, so relax.

→ Because I am here for you, you can relax.

## 5.3　英英辞書の定義を参考にしよう

　以下のような英英辞書に記載されている定義をリテリングで使用するの
もよいですが，生徒に定義を考えさせて，パラフレーズの練習をさせるの
もよいでしょう。

Part 1

operate → to cut open somebody's body in order to remove a part that has a
disease or is damaged

patient → a person who is receiving medical treatment, especially in a hospital

Part 2

motto → a short sentence or phrase that expresses the aims and beliefs of a
person

invent → to produce something that has not existed before

microscope → an instrument used in scientific study for making very small
things look larger so that you can examine them carefully

shave → to cut hair from the skin

Part 3

naughty → behaving badly

mentor → an experienced person who advises and helps somebody with less
experience over a period of time

knowledge → the information, understanding and skills that you get through education or experience

Part 4

correct → to make something right or accurate

priority → something that you think is more important than other things

## 5.4　検定教科書付属のパラフレーズデータを使用しよう

　検定教科書付属のパラフレーズデータの中で，特にパラフレーズをさせたい語句，節，文に対して，空欄を作成して，その空欄に入るものを考えさせることでパラフレーズ力を高めることができます。空欄の先頭の文字を提示してヒントを与えてもよいでしょう。以下は検定教科書付属のパラフレーズデータです。下線部はパラフレーズされた箇所です。

［Part 1］　※ Part 1 のみ空欄にする箇所を（　　　　）にしています。

　Doctor Takanori Fukushima is a Japanese brain surgeon (working) in the United States. People (call) Dr. Fukushima "the man with the Hands of God." He is also (called) "the Samurai Doctor," "Black Jack," and "the Last Hope." Why do people (give) him such names?

　By 2007, Dr. Fukushima had operated on more than 20,000 people (all over the world). (A great number of) these patients had (bad) brain tumors that other doctors did not (want to touch). It is very (surprising) that Dr. Fukushima has had nearly 100 percent success in operations that (are so hard). He does (more than) 600 operations each year around the world, and more than 500 people are waiting for Dr. Fukushima's help even now. From (these facts) we can know what (a great surgeon he is).

［Part 2］

　"Everything for the good of the patients" is the motto of Dr. Fukushima.

In order to do <u>finer</u> operations, Dr. Fukushima invented the "keyhole" method. In <u>usual operations on the brain</u>, doctors cut open a <u>big part</u> of the patient's skull. <u>Doing this is a big risk for the patient.</u> The "keyhole" method <u>cuts down the risk</u> and makes operations <u>a lot more</u> successful. <u>This</u> method <u>needs just</u> a small hole <u>in</u> the patient's head. <u>The hole is more or less the same size as a one-yen coin.</u> Through this "keyhole" and <u>using</u> a surgical microscope, Dr. Fukushima can reach the tumor in the patient's brain.

Dr. Fukushima's motto <u>reaches</u> beyond his operations. For example, before one operation, a young doctor <u>cut the hair off the head of a female patient.</u> <u>When</u> Dr. Fukushima saw <u>a few</u> cuts on <u>the head of the patient</u>, he said to the doctor, "What on earth have you done to this patient? Look at this poor woman! After the operation, she will <u>look at her face in a mirror</u> and feel sad <u>because there are</u> so many cuts on her head. You must <u>think of ALL THINGS for the patient's good!</u>"

[Part 3]

<u>Dr. Fukushima was born in 1942.</u> <u>His father was a priest of the Meiji Shrine.</u> In elementary school <u>he was very good at his studies, but he also behaved very badly.</u> <u>One time in the winter</u>, for example, he <u>got</u> the chimney pipe from the coal stove and <u>made</u> a clever trap. When his teacher opened <u>the classroom door</u>, the chimney pipe fell and black soot covered her. In the third year he <u>was made to</u> change schools <u>because he behaved so badly</u>.

<u>During the years he was in junior high school</u>, Dr. Fukushima did not think <u>very much</u> about his future. When he was <u>a high school student</u>, <u>the uncle he liked most</u>, a respected doctor, <u>said to him that he should</u> become a doctor and help sick people. Dr. Fukushima decided to follow <u>his uncle's advice</u> and began to study hard.

<u>Some</u> years later, he <u>entered</u> the School of Medicine at the University of Tokyo, and <u>chose</u> the field of <u>brain surgery</u>. At the University of Tokyo, he met his mentor, Professor Keishi Sano. Dr. Fukushima says, "Professor

Sano <u>knows a lot about</u> various sciences and arts as well as medicine. <u>Also</u>, he loves his students and cares <u>greatly</u> about them. I have always <u>wanted</u> to become like Professor Sano."

[Part 4]

Today, as <u>a surgeon with much experience</u>, Dr. Fukushima teaches students and younger doctors <u>his ways of operating</u>. One time, <u>when they were</u> doing an operation, a younger doctor made a mistake. <u>When</u> Dr. Fukushima noticed <u>the mistake</u>, <u>he took away the doctor's surgical knife</u>. <u>Then he continued to lecture</u> the doctor for six hours while he was correcting the mistake. <u>If he sees that younger doctors are working</u> too slowly, <u>he always shows them how to work faster and with greater care</u>. Dr. Fukushima is a strict teacher but the younger doctors <u>have great respect for</u> him. They know that the patient is always <u>the most important person for him</u>.

Dr. Fukushima is very gentle and <u>kind to</u> his patients. Even before <u>hard</u> operations, he always says to the patients, "I am here <u>to help you</u>, so relax. You are <u>safe with me</u>." He <u>is not trying to</u> show off his skills. He <u>just</u> wants <u>each</u> of his patients to feel at peace. Dr. Fukushima says, "When I see <u>patients of mine</u> smile after successful operations, I <u>am really happy</u>. I <u>am sure</u> I have found <u>my reason for</u> living."

## 5.5　AET によるパラフレーズを使用しよう

　検定教科書付属のパラフレーズデータに加えて，勤務校で教えている AET に本文をパラフレーズしてもらうことで，パラフレーズ指導に使用できる教材がもう１つ増えます。AET に既習の文法項目をできるだけ入れてもらうこともできるので大変有益な教材となるでしょう。以下は AET によるパラフレーズです。下線部はパラフレーズされた箇所です。

[Part 1]

Doctor Takanori Fukishima is a Japanese neurosurgeon <u>known by many</u>

names in the United States. He is called names such as "the man with the Hands of God," "the Samurai Doctor," and "the Last Hope." Dr. Fukushima had operated on more than 20,000 patients all over the world by 2007. He has been almost 100% successful in difficult operations on serious brain tumors, proving that he is a great and amazing doctor.

[Part 2]

Dr. Fukushima's motto, "everything for the good of the patient", is for both during and outside of operations. He developed the "keyhole" method, which only needs a small hole, making operations less risky and more successful. He also uses his motto outside of the operating room, thinking about how a patient will look and feel after an operation. Dr. Fukushima teaches his methods and motto to future doctors.

[Part 3]

Dr. Fukushima was a very bright, but naughty boy in elementary school. He played tricks on his teachers and had to change schools. This behavior changed in high school and he began to study hard when his uncle advised him to be a doctor and help people. Later, when he was a medical student in neurosurgery at the University of Tokyo, he met his mentor, Professor Keiji Sano. He is a man who is very knowledgeable, loves his students, and is someone who Dr. Fukushima wanted to be like.

[Part 4]

Now, Dr. Fukushima teaches his methods to students and other doctors. He teaches them to work well while keeping the patient as the top priority. Even though he is a strict teacher, the younger doctors greatly respect him. When it comes to his patients, Dr. Fukushima is very gentle and kind. He tries his best to help all of his patients to feel at peace with him. He believes that he found his purpose in life by helping his patients.

# 第5章のまとめ

〈リテリングの手順〉

（Ⅰ）内容理解
（Ⅱ）音読による内在化
（Ⅲ）発話情報の選定
（Ⅳ）**英語への変換**
（Ⅴ）発話

●発話する英語の質には，「英語テキストの原文と同じかほぼ同じ」，「数ヵ所だけをパラフレーズしたもの」，「多くの箇所をパラフレーズしたもの」という3つの種類があり，生徒の英語習熟度に応じて，どの種類を求めるのかを判断する。

●パラフレーズ力を育成するために，本文の語彙や表現を言い換えさせる指導がある。まずは，個人でどのように言い換えることができるのかを考えさせてから，ペアやグループで共有することで，多種多様な言い換えに触れることができる。

●文の構造を言い換えさせる指導は，単に語彙を言い換えるパラフレーズよりは，本文の言語形式をかなり異なる言語形式に変えることができ，パラフレーズの醍醐味を経験させることができる。文の構造を言い換えさせる指導では，既習の文法項目を使用することが多いので，既習の文法項目を復習することにもなる。

●英英辞書の定義を利用した指導もパラフレーズ力を高める指導となる。語彙リストに英英辞書の定義を追加するのがよい。また，パラフレーズさせたい語彙は空欄にしておいて，生徒に英語で定義を考えさせるのもよい。

●最近の検定教科書には，付属のデータ集の中に本文をパラフレーズしたデータが置かれていることが多いので，それを使用して，空欄を作成し，その空欄に入る語彙，表現，文を考えさせる指導は有益なパラフレーズ指導となる。

●勤務校の AET に頼んで，本文をパラフレーズしてもらうことで，英語話者視点のパラフレーズ例を提示することができる。また，特定の語彙，表現，文法項目をパラフレーズに入れてもらうこともでき，指導のねらいに応じたカスタマイズのパラフレーズ例を作成することができるので，有益な教材となる。

## 第6章

# リテリングの手順（V）：発話

　リテリングの最後の手順は，英語を発声することです。発声というと，発音，アクセントなどの音声的観点からの指導は当然必要ですが，本書では音声的観点には触れずに，発声するときの形態についての解説を行うことにします。

## 6.1　口頭と筆記のどちらで行うのか

　表6-1を見てください。リテリングの方法は，既述したように口頭によるものと筆記によるものがあります。学校現場では，スピーキング力を高めたければ口頭を選択し，ライティング力を高めたければ筆記を選択することになりますが，両方を取り入れることもできます。例えば，口頭によるリテリングを行ってから，筆記によるリテリングを行うことが考えられます。口頭の場合だと文字として残らないために，自分の発話がどのようなものであったのかを後で確認することが難しいです。発話を録音するICレコーダーがあれば振り返りが可能ですが，生徒と同じ数のICレコーダーが整備されている学校は少ないのが現状だと思います（スマホを使用するという方法もありますが，授業中にスマホを使用させることに抵抗があるかもしれません）。そこで，口頭によるリテリングの後に，筆記によるリテリングを行うことで，自分が筆記した英文と本文との比較が可能となり，本文の中で，どの英文が再生され，どの英文が再生されなかったのかを検証することができるだけでなく，誤りの発見や修正を行うこともできます。

| リテリングの方法 | 対象技能 | リテリング<br>データの収集方法 |
|---|---|---|
| 口頭 | スピーキング | IC レコーダー |
| 筆記 | ライティング | 筆記再生 |

表6-1　リテリングの方法によって生じる違い

さらにリテリングの方法である「話す」・「書く」と，インプットの種類である「読む」・「聞く」を組み合わせると，以下の4つの指導パターンに分類できます。目的に応じて，技能統合の組み合わせを選択することができます。

| 1 | 読んで→話す | 3 | 聞いて→話す |
|---|---|---|---|
| 2 | 読んで→書く | 4 | 聞いて→書く |

# 6.2　個人，ペア，グループのどの形態で行うのか

リテリングを行うときの形態は，表6-2のように4種類あります。

| 個人 | 自信を持ってリテリングができるように何度も行う。 |
|---|---|
| ペア | 個人練習の成果をペアで確認する。 |
| グループ | より多くの生徒の前で発表させ，発表する経験を積ませる。 |
| 全体発表 | 最も上手な発表者に模範となるリテリングをさせる。 |

表6-2　リテリングの形態

徐々に自信を高めていくことを考慮すると，「個人→ペア→グループ→全体発表」の流れで指導するのが望ましいでしょう。個人でのリテリングは，その後に続くペア，グループ，全体によるリテリングのための個人練習として位置付け，この段階で十分に練習させることで，自信を持ってリテリングができるように指導します。ペアで行うときには，生徒Aがリテリングをするならば，生徒Bはそのリテリングの聞き手になり，生徒Aのリテリングが滞ったときには，手がかりを与えるなどの役割を担当さ

せます。グループで行うときには，例えば，4人グループで，1課のパートが4つある場合なら，ジグソーリーディングの手法を用いて，それぞれの生徒にパートを割り当てて役割分担をさせることで，インフォメーションギャップを生み出すことも考えられます。インフォメーションギャップのあるリテリングの場合，聞き手にはメモを取りながら聞くように指導し，リテリングの後で，話し手に質問をすることで，話し手と聞き手のインタラクションを生み出すこともできます。また，筆記によるリテリングをさせ，それを他の生徒と交換し，フィードバックをもらうことで，協同学習を取り入れた指導を行うこともできます。

## 6.3　ペアやグループによるリテリングの種類

　個人でのリテリングはあくまで個人練習であり，全体発表でのリテリングはモデルの提示という位置付けなので，これらのリテリングのバリエーションは少ないですが，ペアやグループによるリテリングでは，いくつかのバリエーションが考えられます。以下は *Genius English Communication I Revised*（大修館書店，平成29年度発行）の LESSON 6　Willpower and Sleep の Part 1 を題材とした指導例です（※本文は 2.1 を参照）。

### 6.3.1　1人1文リテリング

　ペアなら交互で，グループなら1人ひとりが，同じ手がかりを見ながら1文ずつ順番にリテリングをします。1人ずつ順番に発話しなければならないので，責任感が生まれ，この活動の前に行う個人練習では熱心に練習する姿が見られるでしょう。

【活動の流れ】（3人1組の場合）

> 〈手がかり〉
> ability / emotion / influence / happier / improve / place / effective / insights / create / gaining

A：Willpower is the important <u>ability</u> to control our attention, <u>emotions</u>, and desires.

B：It <u>influences</u> our lives in many ways.

C：People who use willpower more than others are <u>happier</u> and healthier.

A：If you want to <u>improve</u> your lives, willpower is not a bad <u>place</u> to start.

B：In order to find <u>effective</u> ways to develop willpower, we can rely on new <u>insights</u> from science.

C：A number of ways have been found to help us <u>create</u> healthy habits for <u>gaining</u> willpower.

## 6.3.2　繰り返しリテリング

　ペアなら交互で，グループなら1人ひとりが，同じ手がかりを見ながら1文ずつ順番にリテリングをしますが，自分の順番より前に話された内容についても，再度話してから，続きの1文を話します。再度話すときには，他の生徒が使用した表現を使う必要はなく，自分の言葉で話すことができるので，グループ内で他の生徒によるパラフレーズを学ぶことができます。

【活動の流れ】（4人1組の場合）

〈手がかり〉→ 6.3.1 に同じ

A：Willpower is the important <u>ability</u> to control our attention, <u>emotions</u>, and desires.

B：Willpower is the important ability to control our attention, emotions, and desires. It <u>influences</u> our lives in many ways.

C：Willpower is the important ability to control our attention, emotions, and desires. It influences our lives in many ways. People who use willpower more than others are <u>happier</u> and healthier.

D：Willpower is the important ability to control our attention, emotions, and desires. It influences our lives in many ways. People who use willpower more than others are happier and healthier. If you want to <u>improve</u> your lives, willpower is not a bad <u>place</u> to start.

### 6.3.3　ジグソーリテリング

　複数のグループ（「ホームグループ」と呼びます）を作り，グループのメンバーは，それぞれが異なるパートを担当します。例えば，1課が4パート構成なら，4人グループを作らせて，Aにパート1，Bにパート2，Cにパート3，Dにパート4を割り当てます。メンバーはそれぞれ，自分の担当パートだけを読んで内容理解をします。その後，同じパートを担当する4人が集まり，教え合いをしながら内容理解をさらに深めます（「エキスパートグループ」と呼びます）。「ホームグループ」と「エキスパートグループ」のイメージとしては図6-1のようになります。また，エキスパートグループ内でリテリングの練習と発表を行い，お互いにフィードバックをします。その後，ホームグループに戻り，各自の担当したパートの内容についてリテリングを行います。そのときに，自分の担当パート以外のリテリングを聞くときには，聞きながら内容に関するメモをとらせます。その後，各パートに対して5問程度のTF質問が書かれたプリントを配布し，自分が聞き取ったメモに基づいて，個人でそのTF質問に答えます。聞き取っていないことについて推測で答えないようにします。全員が解答したら，正答を伝え，ホームグループ内でパートごとに集計を行い，自分の担当パートの得点の合計，つまり，リテリングの成功度合いを確認します。すべてのグループの中で，パートごとに一番得点の高かった生徒をベストリテラーとして発表してもよいでしょう。4パートなら4人のベストリテラーにはリテリングをさせ，他の生徒にベストリテラーによるモデルリテリングを聞かせるのもよいでしょう。ジグソーリテリングを行うときには，学習していない語彙は聞き取れないので，事前に1課全体の語彙指導が必要となります。

〈ジグソーリテリングの指導手順〉

1　1課全体の語彙指導を行います。
2　ホームグループを作り，担当パートを割り当てます。
3　個人で担当パートの内容理解をさせます。
4　エキスパートグループを作り，同じパートを担当する者同士で教え合

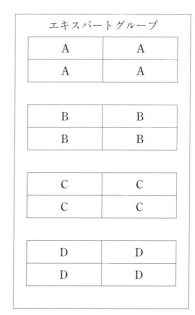

| ホームグループ | |
|:---:|:---:|
| A | B |
| D | C |

| A | B |
|:---:|:---:|
| D | C |

| A | B |
|:---:|:---:|
| D | C |

| A | B |
|:---:|:---:|
| D | C |

| エキスパートグループ | |
|:---:|:---:|
| A | A |
| A | A |

| B | B |
|:---:|:---:|
| B | B |

| C | C |
|:---:|:---:|
| C | C |

| D | D |
|:---:|:---:|
| D | D |

**図6-1　ジグソーリテリングのイメージ**

　いをしながら内容理解をさらに深めさせます。

5　エキスパートグループ内でリテリングの個人練習，発表，フィード
　バックをさせます。

6　ホームグループに戻らせ，ホームグループ内で担当パートのリテリン
　グをパートの順番で行わせます。そのときに，自分の担当パート以外
　については，他の生徒のリテリングを聞きながらメモをとらせます。

7　TF質問プリントを配布し，グループ内で相談しないで，自分の聞き
　取ったメモに基づいて，TF質問に答えさせます。そのときに，Tと
　Fだけでなく，リテリングで発話されなかった情報については，情報
　なし（NI = No Information）の記号も使用させ，推測で答えないよう
　にさせます。もし，自分の担当パートのTF質問に答えられないよう
　なら，内容理解の段階でつまずいていることになります。

8　ホームグループ内でパートごとに得点を集計させて，自分のリテリン
　グの成功度合いを確認させます。

9　得点に基づいて，パートごとにベストリテラーや，総得点に基づいた
　ベストグループを発表します。

〈ジグソーリテリングを経験した生徒の感想〉
○他の人と助け合いながら，英語だけでリテリングをして相手に伝えられ
　たことが自信になりました。今後もまたやりたいです。リスニング力が
　足りないのでそれも頑張りたいです。
○自分の力でまとめて話すのが難しかった。何回も読むことで内容がよく
　分かったし，それを伝えるために伝え方の工夫を考えて実行することが
　できてよかった。
○パートごとやグループごとで得点を競い合うなど，楽しみながら学習で
　きた。内容を理解するだけでなく，他の人にそれを伝える力も向上した。
　ジグソーリテリングはかなり難しかったが，それだけ力が付いたと思う。
○ジグソーリテリングは相手に分かりやすくスピーキングをする力や相手
　が話す内容をリスニングする力が鍛えられると思いました。グループで
　の学習は個人とは違い，コミュニケーション力も向上するのでとても良
　いと思います。
○他の人のパートを聞くときに分からない単語がないように勉強しようと
　思えたり，自分のパートをしっかり理解しようとやる気が出たのが良
　かった。伝えやすいように文を言い換える工夫をしたりして英語力が高
　まる。

## 6.4　帯活動にリテリングを取り入れよう

　検定教科書を用いたリテリングでは，「語彙指導→内容理解→音読指導
→リテリング」が基本的な指導の流れですが，既習レッスンを用いて，授
業の始めに帯活動としてリテリングをさせるのもよいでしょう。以下は，
リテリングを取り入れた帯活動を行う利点です。

　（1）英語の授業に臨む動機を高めることができる。
　例えば，授業の最初に既習レッスンを題材としたリテリングを行うこと

で，スピーキング活動から授業を始めることができるので，「英語の授業が始まったぞ！」という気持ちを持たせることができます。また，ペアの形態を用いて，パートナーのリテリングを聞いた後に，即興質問を1つ言わなければならないといった条件を追加することで，インタラクションを生み出すこともできます。

（2）スピーキングの機会を増やすことができる。

毎授業の始めにリテリングを行うことでスピーキングの機会を増やすことができます。同じレッスンを用いて何度もリテリングをさせると，繰り返しの効果により，質と量の2つの観点において，上達させることができます。

（3）既習レッスンの復習をすることができる。

既習レッスンを扱ったリテリングをすることで，既習レッスンの復習をすることができます。リテリングの準備段階では，再度，本文を読むことになり，既習語彙や表現を復習でき，また，それらを繰り返し使用することになるので定着につながります。どの既習レッスンのリテリングをしたいのかを生徒に選択させることで，より自主的なリテリングにもなります。

## 6.5　高度なリテリングをしてみよう

読んだり，聞いたりした内容について伝えるだけに留まらず，自己表現を追加することでリテリングを高度化させることができます。以下は，リテリングを高度化するためのアイデアです。

（1）本文に関する自分の意見を追加する［→ 6.5.1］
（2）登場人物の気持ちを推測して追加する［→ 6.5.2］
（3）本文の続きを推測して追加する［→ 6.5.3］
（4）ダイアローグ・リテリングを行う［→ 6.5.4］
（5）プレゼンテーション・リテリングを行う［→ 6.5.5］

## 6.5.1 本文に関する自分の意見を追加する

　以下は，*CROWN English Communication I New Edition*（三省堂，平成29年度発行）の LESSON 5 Food Bank を題材として，リテリングの最後に本文に関する自分の意見を追加した生徒の作品です。

LESSON 5  Food Bank

Food banks collect surplus food from companies, supermarkets, and farmers and give it to people who need help. Charles E. McJilton started the first food bank in Japan, Second Harvest Japan（2HJ）.

［Part 1］

　In 1991 I was a university exchange student living in a part of Tokyo where there were many day laborers. When the economy went down, they could not find jobs. I often saw them sleeping on the streets. Their lives were not easy. Many men became alcoholics. Stopping drinking is not easy, but people can change their lives; it is never too late.

　Several years later, I decided to make a self-help center. Without the right "tools"（an address, a phone number, a place to store things and take a bath）, it is hard to get off the streets. This center would give people the "tools" to help themselves. However, by 1997 I had found that there was something missing inside of me. I had a lot of "head knowledge" about homelessness, but lacked "heart knowledge."

［Part 2］

　From January 1997 until April 1998, I lived along the Sumida River in a cardboard house. This experience changed me. I saw the world with the eyes of a homeless person. I experienced homelessness and saw hungry people every day. To my surprise, my neighbors did not lose hope. They helped me in many different ways. Many did some kind of work, such as collecting cans. I kept working in a Japanese company without telling my co-workers where I lived. Every day I could see that people are people; it doesn't matter if they work in a company or live on the streets.

The government reports that more than 15 percent of Japanese people live below the relative poverty line. For the elderly this number is more than 20 percent. Approximately 2.3 million people in Japan do not have enough safe, nutritious food each day. I remember a time when we received a call from a single mother who had two small children. That day she had to ask the older child to give up a meal so that the smaller one could eat. Such things happen every day, even in Japan.

[Part 3]

The first food bank started in the U.S. in 1967. In Japan, we started our activities in 2000 and became an NPO called Second Harvest Japan in March 2002. Our name comes from the idea of "harvesting" surplus food.

We not only give food to people who need it, but we also help companies save money. In 2010, we "harvested" over 500 million yen worth of food. Companies saved 80 million yen because they did not have to throw away the food that they could not sell.

Trust is very important in our work. When you have trust, food and financial support naturally follow. We never go to a company and say, "Can you give us food or money?" We think of them as equal partners. We tell them about our activities and ask them, "Is there anything we can do together?"

NPO's are still new in Japan. As NPO's grow and become more professional, people will see that they can play a bigger role in society. Just wanting to do something good is not enough. The important thing is how you run your NPO. Second Harvest Japan is unique because we deal with both business and welfare.

[Part 4]

"Helping" others is not easy. Sometimes we send the wrong message when we say, "Can I help you?" We mean well, but we sometimes send the message, "You are not OK; you need to change." I would rather think of it this way: "I see you have a flat tire on your bike. I have some tools and patches here if you want to use them. I can also stay around while you fix your bike if you want company." This is what I learned from my experience along the Sumida River.

My work is my "vote" on what kind of society I want to live in. Food is also a "tool." I want to live in a society where there is a way to get these "tools" to the people who need them. I don't think of my work as "helping" people, but rather matching up surplus food with those who can use it. I am passionate about making these matches. It is what makes my job so much fun.

---

生徒作品A ※下線部は生徒の意見です。

Charles E. Mc Jilton started the first food bank in Japan, Second Harvest Japan. What is a food bank? It is an organization collecting surplus food and giving it to people needing help.

He first came to Japan in 1991 as an exchange student and saw the poor in this rich country. Six years ago, he tried living along the Sumida River in a cardboard house, working in a Japanese company. To see the world with the eyes of a homeless person, he did it. Generally speaking, a homeless person is a homeless person. They are different from us. But, he could see that people are people.

He thought about how to solve the poverty problem. And he started Second harvest Japan. It is NPO. Its name comes from the idea of "harvesting" surplus. They can give food to people needing it, helping companies save money. So they deal with both business and welfare.

But of course, "to help" others is not easy. Because some people don't receive the right message. For example, in being said, "Can I help you?" some people receive "You are not OK; you need to change." So they hope that we understand their job is to match up surplus food with people who can use it.

Reading this story, I thought that his activity was very wonderful. It is difficult for us to take actions even though we have feelings. I want to be a man that can do it. I also thought that this poverty problem is not somebody else's problem. We can start with small actions. For example, not to waste food, to raise funds, and to help each other. And the most important thing is never to give up. To solve this problem is difficult, but there are many people acting like him. I hope that we will solve this problem.

生徒作品 B　※下線部は生徒の意見です。

Food bank is a self-help center which collects surplus food from companies. It was made by Charles E. Mc Jilton.

He often saw people who were suffering and didn't have a job to work at . Then he thought they can still change their lives. Several years later, he decided to make a self-help center. Needless to say, they need "tools." And he realized that "head knowledge" and "heart knowledge" are important. He tried living along the Sumida River in a cardboard house. To his surprise, his neighbors did not lose hope. He learned that it doesn't matter where to work.

The first food bank started in the U.S. in 1967. Working in Japan started in 2000. Food bank also help companies to save money. It enables companies not to suffer from throwing away the food that they could not sell. So, they helped a lot and can save money. In his work, everyone thinks of companies as equal partners. So, trust is very important. NPO's are still new in Japan. NPO's are still new in Japan. But as NPO grow and become more professional, people will understand his efforts.

Helping others is not easy. And, his trust work is his "vote" on what kind of society he wants to live in. He wants to live in a society where there is a way to get these "tools" to the people who need them. He thinks that his work is matching up surplus food with those who can use it. And he finds his own job fun.

If I have a chance, I want to join this work. I want to give them my surplus food. I'm very glad if my present becomes a little helpful. He thinks that his job is "a tool to help people." I think it is true. Because his jobs help everybody who needs everything. To tell the truth, my dream is to be a person who can help the health of everyone in Japan or the world. So, his job is an attractive one for me.

## 6.5.2　登場人物の気持ちを推測して追加する

「登場人物の気持ちを推測する」というのは，本文の登場人物の心情等を推測して，リテリングに追加するもので，主に物語文を扱うときに行うことができます。本文の内容に基づいて，自由な発想で推測して表現できるところにこの活動の楽しさがあります。事前に，「あなただったらこの状況でどのようなことを考えますか。」といった質問を生徒に投げかけて，ペアやグループで考え，発表させた後で，リテリングに追加させるのもよいでしょう。

## 6.5.3　本文の続きを推測して追加する

「本文の続きを推測する」というのは，本文にある物語の続きを自由に推測し，リテリングに追加したり，物語のエンディングを全く異なる内容に変えたりするもので，主に物語文を扱うときに行うことができます。また，本文の内容によっては，「本文の続き」ではなく，「本文の冒頭部分」を自由に推測することも可能です。「登場人物の気持ちを推測する」と「物語の続きを推測する」は，別々に行うことができますが，両方とも同時に扱うこともできます。以下は，*Compass English Communication I Revised*（大修館書店，平成 29 年度発行）の Supplementary Readings 1 の本文をもとにして「登場人物の気持ちを推測する」と「物語の続きを推測する」の両方を扱った指導用プリントです。

エヌ氏が購入したロボットの巧妙なしかけとは…。

"This is the best robot in the world," the doctor explained proudly. "It can do anything. This is the perfect *companion."

"Then please sell it to me," Mr. N, a *wealthy man, replied. "I'm planning to go to my private island, and I want to use it there."

"It's very useful," said the doctor.

Mr. N paid a lot of money for it and took it with him. He planned to stay on the island for a whole month.

"Now I can *take it easy and rest. By the way, I'm feeling hungry."

"Very good, sir," answered the robot. It immediately prepared a meal and served it.

Mr. N ate the food.

"It's delicious! What a great robot!" he said.

The robot also washed the dishes, cleaned the house, and repaired Mr. N's old watch. It even *entertained him with funny stories. It was the perfect *servant, and Mr. N was enjoying himself.

Two days later, however, something went wrong. The robot suddenly stopped working. Mr. N shouted at it, but that didn't help. He asked it the reason, but he got no reply.

"Oh dear, it must be *out of order."

Mr. N had to prepare his own meals, but suddenly the robot started to work again.

"I *suppose I must give it a rest now and then."


However, the next day, the robot stopped working again and ran away. Mr. N ran after it, but he was unable to catch it. Finally, he was able to bring it back. Then, when he gave it an *order, it did its work without any problems.

Mr. N *scratched his head and thought to himself, "I can't understand it." However, he couldn't ask the doctor about it.

Every day, the robot did something *unexpected. It even suddenly started shouting. It *chased Mr. N, and he had to run away! He climbed a tree and *hid in it. Finally, the robot *calmed down.

"It must be crazy! What an *absurd robot!"

In this way a month passed, and Mr. N went back to the city.

He immediately went to the doctor to *complain.

"I had a terrible time. The robot broke down every day and did crazy things!"

"It's all right," the doctor answered calmly.

"What's all right?"

"Listen.

（この空欄に，物語の続きを書く）

〈*が付いた語彙〉

| | | | |
|---|---|---|---|
| companion 仲間 | wealthy 裕福な | take it easy のんびりする | |
| entertain 〜を楽しませる | servant 使用人・召使い | | |
| out of order 故障して | suppose 〜だと思う | order 命令 | |
| scratch(ed) 〜をかく・こする | unexpected 予期されていない | | |
| chase(d) 〜を追いかける | hid ＜ hide 隠れる | calm down 落ち着く | |
| absurd ばかな | complain 不平を言う | | |

①下線部におけるロボットの気持ちを自由に英語で表現してください。

②本文の最後にある Listen. の後に続く医者の言葉を自由に英語で表現してください。

〈質問①における生徒の英語〉

● I don't want to be your servant. I have my feelings, but he doesn't realize that. So, I decide to run away in order to do what I want to do. Please don't run after me! Please give me free!

● I have been used by Mr.N day by day, so I am tired of that. I don't like to be servant. I want to enjoy my time. I don't want to work any more.

● I don't want to work in his house. He is very lazy man. He should do something on his own. If I left his house, he would work. I won't go back to his house until he starts working.

● I want to be your companion. However, you don't do anything for me. You seem to be a servant employer. I'm too tired to help you, so please let me free. I never want to see your face.

● I don't want to move any more because I was forced to work in everything by Mr. N such as washing the dishes, cleaning the house, repairing his old watch and so on. I think that some of them should be done on his own.

● I can do anything, but I don't want to work for him. The reason is that he asks me to do everything. He is using me without thinking about my heart, so I dislike him.

● I felt disappointed with my life here. I was only allowed to work for Mr.N. I felt bad, so I don't want to work. I decided to leave from Mr. N. I hoped that I would be free as soon as possible.

〈質問②における生徒の英語〉

● Probably the robot wanted to enjoy his life. He didn't want to become a servant but your friend. You should understand that he has a heart even if he is a robot.

● This robot is not the perfect servant but the perfect companion. He has his own feelings and intentions. It is natural that he broke down because of your many orders. If you want to get along with the robot, you should treat him as your friend.

● The robot has his own emotions. So, he feel happy, sad, tired, surprised, and angry. Now he is sad and angry. He didn't just want to work. He wanted to enjoy island life together with you. You should have regarded the robot as companion. In fact, you regarded the robot as servant. That is the reason the robot acted in such a way.

● Certainly, I said, "This is the best robot in the world." But actually, I programed it to reflect your heart. If you take silly action, the robot imitate it. You should learn from this experience. When you can understand it, your life become better.

● The robot is the same as human. The robot feels happy, sad, and hungry like human. If you let the robot do things that you don't want to do, the robot will feel uncomfortable.

● I think you wanted to be happy, so you bought the robot. Certainly, the robot was the perfect robot. It means he has his mind like a human. Probably, you order robot many times. It made him angry. I think you can't buy happiness, but you did it. It brought about this situation.

● The robot work according to your personality. If you use it without thinking about its heart, it wouldn't follow your orders. And if you use it five times, it suddenly stop working. Then it thinks whether it want to work or not.

● This robot is made to be similar to his owner. If the owner is good, this robot become good. But if the owner is lazy, it become lazy. This is why I said "This is the perfect companion."

● The robot can't work without receiving praise from someone. So, if you don't praise the robot, it don't work and do something strange. The robot teach you the importance of gratitude that you forget.

## 6.5.4 ダイアローグ・リテリングを行う

「ダイアローグ・リテリング」とは，本文の内容を会話形式に変えて，リテリングを行うものです。以下は，*CROWN English Communication I New Edition*（三省堂，平成 29 年度発行）の LESSON 5 Food Bank を題材として，筆記による「ダイアローグ・リテリング」を行った生徒の作品です（※本文は 6.5.1 を参照）。

生徒作品 A

※下線部は生徒が考えた質問とその応答であり，原文には存在しないものです。

I ：Mr. McJilton, thank you so much for taking time for this interview. I know that you started the first food bank in Japan. Why did you make it?

M：When I saw people who could not find jobs sleeping on the streets in 1991, I wanted to give them "tools" (an address, a phone number, a place to store things and take a bath) in order to change their lives.

I ：What did you need to make it?

M：To get "heart knowledge" about homelessness. I had a lot of "head knowledge" but lacked "heart knowledge."

I ：Specifically, what are "head knowledge" and "heart knowledge"?

M："Head knowledge is data that is mainly expressed numerically. For example, approximately 2.3 million people in Japan do not have enough safe, nutritious food each day, and only one of two children can eat food. However, "heart knowledge" is something you do not know until you actually experience homelessness. For example, homeless people did not lose hope, they help each other, and they have jobs such as collecting cans.

I ：I see. You have experienced homelessness, haven't you? How did you feel when you got "heart knowledge"?

M：Yes, I have. I felt people are people; it doesn't matter if they work in a company or live on the streets.

I ：Is that so? And you started your activities in 2000 and became an NPO called Second Harvest Japan in March 2002. Why is it called like that?

M：Its name comes from the idea of "harvesting" surplus food. We not only give food to people who need it, but we also help companies save money. In other words, we deal with both business and welfare.

I ：It is great! What is important about doing business?

M：It is trust. When we go to the company, we don't ask people to help. We propose to work with them. It is important to not only want to do something good, but also play a bigger role in society.

I ：What should you be careful of when engaging with people?

M：It is to avoid sending the wrong message. I try to tell people in need my intention firmly, because there may be a misunderstanding.

I ：Wow…! What do you think about your work?

M：I think it is my vote on what kind of society I want to live in. I don't think of my work as "helping people" but I am doing my job to bring food and people together. It is interesting.

I ：<u>Thank you very much for your time and for sharing your ideas with us. Finally, what is the way to make a peaceful world for you?</u>

M：<u>It is to consider your partner. And we don't do something for others, but we help others for ourselves.</u>

生徒作品 B

※下線部は生徒が考えた質問とその応答であり，原文には存在しないものです。

I ：You made the first food bank in the world, didn't you? For what purpose did you start a business?

M：Yes. When I came to Tokyo as an exchange student, I saw a lot of day laborers. To make matters worse,
they also became alcoholics. Looking at this situation, I thought that I could not help creating something for homeless people. I made a self-help center. This is the beginning.

I ：Do you have any other stories?

M：To tell the truth, I have lived in a cardboard house. At that time, I was surprised. Homeless people were finding jobs that they could do without losing hope. In addition, they helped me to try something. At that time, I was able to notice that all people are the same. I still remember having lived in a cardboard house.

I ：Approximately 2.3 million people in Japan don't have enough safe and nutritious meals now. Are you planning to do something about this situation?

M：We established an NPO called Second Harvest Japan in 2002 and give food to those who need it and help entrepreneurs save money. So, I would like to work with more companies to make the world have fewer homeless people.

I ：<u>Finally, please give message to modern people.</u>

M：<u>Everyone thinks that there are many people who ,by all means, avoid seeing homeless people. Why not turn your attention to that problem? You can learn from it. There must be something you feel. I look forward to having the future without such problems.</u>

## 6.5.5　プレゼンテーション・リテリングを行う

　著者が勤務する高校では，「プレゼンテーション・リテリング」をイベント化しています。クラス内で5人グループを作らせ，そのグループごとに使用している検定教科書の中から，お気に入りのレッスンを選ばせて，そのレッスンの内容についてグループのメンバー全員で協力してリテリングを行います。さらに，そのリテリングには，レッスンの内容に関連する検定教科書の本文には記載されていない情報を追加させています。情報科の教師と協力して，パワーポイントによるスライド作成も行います。本校の普通科は1学年7クラスあり，まずはクラスごとにクラス予選会を行い，クラス代表となる1チームを選抜した後は，大きな会場を借りて，7クラスの代表決勝大会を開催して，表彰までを行っています。

　以下のグループAは，*Revised LANDMARK English Communication I*（啓林館，平成29年度発行）の LESSON 6 Biodiesel Adventure を選択し，関連する情報として，日本のエネルギー事情を追加しています。グループBは，*Revised LANDMARK English Communication I*（啓林館，平成29年度発行）の LESSON 7　Eco-tour on Yakushima を選択し，関連する情報として，屋久島の自然を守っているボランティア活動を追加しています。

LESSON 5　Biodiesel Adventure
［Part 1］

　I am Shusei Yamada, a photojournalist. I drove around the world with "Vasco-5," an eco-friendly car. The car runs on vegetable oil! It carries a machine which makes biodiesel fuel out of used vegetable oil. I did not buy new oil but collected waste oil from people in many countries.

　There were two purposes of this adventure. One purpose was to examine how far I could go with only waste oil. The other purpose was to communicate with people around the world about biodiesel fuel.

　Before beginning my journey, I had worried about one thing. In the world, there are many varieties of vegetable oils such as rapeseed, palm, and olive oil. I was not sure if Vasco-5 could process all of these oils. But some people say the only way to learn is "by doing." So, I started the engine of Vasco-5 in Tokyo on December 5th, 2007.

[Part 2]

After test-driving Vasco-5 in Japan, I sailed across the Pacific Ocean to North America. The first city I visited was Vancouver, Canada. I asked for waste oil in many restaurants and hotels there. However, my requests were often refused because people knew little about biodiesel fuel. That made me feel disappointed. Still, as people heard about my project, they started bringing me waste oil from their homes. It took me a few days to process the oil into biodiesel fuel. After the process was finished, I was able to start on my journey again. When I ran out of fuel, I stopped and asked people for waste oil again.

A month later, I left Vancouver for the US. More and more people helped me on my journey. Some people e-mailed their friends about my project. Surprisingly, when I arrived in their town, they had already collected waste oil for me. In San Francisco, people even held a welcome party for me. I traveled from Los Angeles to the Grand Canyon and then to the East Coast. To save fuel, I had to drive carefully. Vasco-5 and I went across the North American continent and finally arrived in Washington, D.C. on April 19th. Then, Vasco-5 and I got on a ferry for Europe to cross the Atlantic Ocean.

[Part 3]

In June, my journey began again with Vasco-5 in Lisbon, Portugal. I drove Vasco-5 through Spain to Morocco in Africa. I wanted to test-drive Vasco-5 under the very severe conditions of the Sahara Desert. Although the daytime temperature there got as high as 52°C (degrees Celsius), Vasco-5 was able to run without any problem.

Then, I drove back from Africa to Europe the next month and headed for the east end of the Eurasian continent. After visiting several European countries, I arrived in the last country on my journey, Russia, in September. It was very cold there. Even in the daytime, the temperature was below the freezing point. The oil people brought to me there had often frozen. So, I had to heat the oil on the stove before processing it into biodiesel fuel.

On December 1st, 2008, Vasco-5 and I came back to Tokyo by way of Siberia. It took me almost one year to drive 47,853 km (kilometers) around the world.

[Part 4]

Wherever I went, people who heard of Vasco-5 were waiting for me with waste oil. Some people offered me not only oil but also food or a place to stay for free. Others took a day off from work to collect waste oil for me. Moreover, other people supported me so that I could pass through the borders between countries. Since Vasco-5 carried an unusual machine on it, few border officers let me pass through the borders easily. I was moved by the kindness of the people who helped me. Meeting such good people from different races and countries was the most precious gift for me on this journey.

More than 1,000 people offered waste oil to me throughout the journey. My journey proved that I could travel around the world by using waste oil. In fact, Vasco-5 used 6,540 L (liters) of oil to make the journey. Here is a lesson I learned from this adventure: If each of us in the world makes a small effort, we will be able to produce big results.

グループ A

※下線部は生徒たちが追加した本文に関連する情報

We'll give a presentation on our group study. We researched lesson 5. This is the story of Shusei Yamada, who drove all over the world with Vasco-5, an eco-friendly car. The car runs on vegetable oil. In addition, it carries a machine which makes biodiesel fuel out of used vegetable oil. According to him, it took a few days to process the oil into biodiesel fuel. This is the route on which he drove around the world. Like this, there are various kinds of biodiesel. Because used oil can contain various oils, there is variation. According to Lesson 5, fuel had frozen in Siberia. From this, we can understand how these oils are used.

Next, I'll talk about the Japanese energy situation. In Japan, more than 40% of carbon dioxide emissions are discharged when making energy. And Japan has a goal to reduce that by 26% by 2030. So, people are paying attention to new energy sources which don't give off carbon dioxide when supplying energy. There are various kinds of new energy sources. For example, as you all know, there is solar, geothermal , wind and water energy. These energy sources are used by power generators. Also, burning garbage and biomass creates thermal energy. In addition, not only these energy sources are used but also energy from the sea. These energies are eco-friendly. The percentage of energy from new energy sources accounts for 12% of all power generation. This number is not large. And only one quarter of that amount is from non-water sources. That's because it costs a lot and the amount of energy production is not high. However, it is important for the benefit of the earth for us to use this technology.

By the way, have you ever thought about power generation from lightning? A single bolt of lightning makes 2 million volts of energy to 200 million volts of energy and 1000 anpenes to 200,000 anpenes. That is a very big amount. But the time is short. So, if we collect all the lightning around Japan, its electric energy amount can't cover Japan's power consumption. We use 1,000 times more electric power than that! For that reason, power generation from lightning isn't realistic. New energy rate is still small. So we think that it is important to know about new energy and use it well.

LESSON 7  Eco-tour on Yakushima
[Part 1]
Good morning, everyone. Welcome to Yakushima! Thank you very much

for joining our eco-tour. My name is Suzuki Kenta, and I'm your guide for the tour. First, I am going to give you a short orientation. After that, we will start the tour. We'll return to this office tomorrow evening.

By the way, do you know what an "eco-tour" is? It is a trip in which people are asked to be more responsible for the environment. In other words, we need to be more careful not to damage the environment while we're on the tour. Yakushima was registered as Japan's first Natural World Heritage Site in 1993. Since then, the number of tourists to this island has greatly increased. Of course, we're very happy to have so many tourists, but this has caused some problems. For example, plants along some mountain paths have been stepped on and damaged by the tourists. So, before starting the tour, I want all of you to understand the meaning of eco-tours.

[Part 2]

Now we're going to take a look at the land features of Yakushima. This is a picture of the island. Yakushima is a round island which is covered with green forest. It's about 500 km$^2$ (square kilometers). If you compare Yakushima with Tokyo or Osaka, you can understand its size. On the island, there're over 40 mountains which are more than 1,000 m (meters) high. So, Yakushima is called "the Alps of the Sea."

The climate in Yakushima is usually warm and humid throughout the year. The average annual temperature is 20℃ in the areas along the coast and 15℃ in the central area. It is surprising that the temperature can fall below zero in the mountain top area in winter. During this time, it is covered with snow. Yakushima has a lot of rain and it is said that "it rains 35 days a month!" The humidity is high, about 73-75% on average. The annual rainfall is about 4,000 mm (millimeters) in the low-lying areas. In the mountain areas, it's about 8,000-10,000 mm. This climate, along with its land features, has created a unique ecosystem on Yakushima.

[Part 3]

Next, I'll show you the three sites where we are going. Look at this picture. You'll find something mysterious in it. It's Shiratani Unsuikyo, a dense forest with a thick carpet of moss. Have you seen the animated movie, Princess Mononoke? When he was making this movie, Miyazaki Hayao, the director, was strongly inspired by this mysterious forest. We're going to go there this afternoon.

The next picture is Wilson's Stump, a great stump with a diameter of 4.39 m. The inside of the stump is empty, and we can go into it. Surprisingly, we can see some water flowing out of the ground there. You'll also find a small shrine. It is said that this tree was cut down in 1586 by the order of Toyotomi Hideyoshi to build Hokoji-temple. By the way, do you know the reason why it is called Wilson's Stump? It was named after Dr. Wilson, a famous botanist. He was the first person to introduce this stump to the world in 1914. I think you will enjoy this site, too.

[Part 4]

The last picture is, as you all know, Jomon Cedar. It's one of the oldest and largest cedars in Yakushima. It was discovered in 1966. Can you imagine how old and how large it is? It is considered to be 2,000-4,000 years old. Some people say it is 7,200 years old! It is 25.4 m in height and it is 5.2 m in diameter. Tomorrow we will look for this tree on the tour.

In the Edo period, people in Yakushima began to cut down cedars. They had a poor rice crop because there was little land for growing rice there. As a result, they had to offer boards of cedars as nengu (land tax). Fortunately, some cedars over 1,000 years old were left uncut then because they were not suitable for making boards. That's why we can still see them as well as Jomon Cedar!

I'm very sorry to say that we can't touch or get close to Jomon Cedar. We can only look at it from a distance. That's because many tourists stepped on the roots and damaged the tree. This fact makes us think about the meaning of eco-tours.

That's all for the orientation. Do you have any questions?

グループ B

※下線部は生徒たちが追加した本文に関連する情報

We will start the presentation of group C now. First, we will introduce Yakushima. Yakushima is a round island which is covered with green forest. And both the temperature and humidity are high. The unique ecosystem is formed by the land formations and climate. There is a lot of natural scenery. For example, Shiratani Unsuikyo is the stage of Princess Mononoke. Wilson's Stump is a well known Jomon Cedar and a place where we can go into. Because of these things, Yakushima was registered as a Natural World Heritage Site in 1993. Since then, many tourists have visited Yakushima. People in Yakushima seem to be happy, but there are big problems. Plants have been stepped on and damaged by tourists. Because of this, we can't approach the Jomon Cedar to protect it. We felt disappointed, when we learned about this problem.

So, we searched for volunteer activities which protect the nature of Yakushima. The volunteer activities can be grouped into 4 groups. The first is environment protection.

The main activity is removing Okinkeigiku. The second is cleaning the coast. As a result, the coast view is protected. The third is exchanging with foreign students through educational activities to learn about Yakushima. The fourth is the protection of turtles. This activity is setting up a protection group to defend turtles. We also do things to protect sea turtles. There are four rules for watching turtles. First, don't enter the turtle's protective fence. If someone enters it, they can step on turtle eggs and small turtles. Second, don't have camp-fires. Because small turtles see the fire and run into it. So small turtles can be burned to death. Third, don't camp near the ocean. The light you use while camping negatively effects both adult and baby sea turtles. Fourth, don't take sand from the beach. Doing so will decrease the number of areas where sea turtles can lay their eggs. There is a lot you can do to protect nature and animals. We hope that you're going to be interested in Yakushima and volunteer activities through your understanding of our research. That's all for our presentation.

## 6.6 アウトプットⅢの活動を取り入れよう

　アウトプットⅢについて説明するために，リテリングを取り入れた指導モデルを再度確認したいと思います（8ページの表1-2参照）。認知負荷の軽重によって，リプロダクションをアウトプットⅠ，リテリングをアウトプットⅡと位置付けています。リプロダクションやリテリングは本文の内容に関するアウトプットですので，リプロダクションやリテリングの後には，自分の意見や考えについて即興で話したり，書いたりするアウトプットⅢの活動を取り入れたいものです。

### 6.6.1　本文の内容に関連する評価発問をする

　検定教科書を用いたアウトプットⅢの活動例として，レッスンの内容に関連させて自分の意見を述べさせる評価発問というものがあります。以下は，*CROWN English Communication I New Edition*（三省堂，平成29年度発行）の LESSON 4 に関する本文の内容に関連させたパートごとの評価発問の例です。

LESSON 4  Seeing with the Eyes of the Heart
After the first few chords, no one was aware that the pianist was blind. They were aware only of his music. "I want people to listen to me as just one pianist who happens to be blind," he said. The pianist is Tsujii Nobuyuki. His friends call him Nobu.

[Part 1]

When Nobu's parents learned that their son was blind, they were very sad. However, they soon discovered that he had a special talent. When Nobu was two, he heard his mother sing "Jingle Bells." A few minutes later, he surprised her by playing the tune on his toy piano.

As soon as Nobu began taking piano lessons at the age of four, he surprised his teachers with his memory. Nobu is able to read music by touch, but he likes to learn by ear. He listens to a tape recorded for him and remembers what he hears.

The piano is Nobu's great love. He especially likes Debussy, Chopin, and Beethoven. He plays jazz, and once had a chance to meet the popular musician Stevie Wonder. He is also blind from birth.

[Part 2]

At the age of 20, Nobu decided to enter the Van Cliburn International Piano Competition: one of the most famous competitions in the world. It is held every four years in Texas. This event was a turning point in his life. Nobu and his mother flew to Texas. They met their American host family, the Davidsons. They warmly welcomed Nobu and his mother and did their best to make them feel at home. They even prepared a Japanese rice cooker for Nobu and his mother.

Nobu practiced many hours each day during the three weeks of the competition. When he was playing the piano, the beautiful music made Mrs. Davidson cry. "I cry a lot when I hear him play," she said. Even the neighbors loved Nobu's music. They asked the Davidsons to keep the doors and windows of their house open; they wanted to hear Nobu practice every morning.

[Part 3]

The day for giving the prizes arrived. Nobu was among the six finalists. First prize was 20,000 dollars and the chance to go on concert tours all over the world, a dream for any young musician. Everybody waited anxiously as the announcements were made.

First, they named the second-prize winner: a pianist from South Korea who had become one of Nobu's closest friends. And then the first-prize winner was announced: a 19-year-old pianist from China. Nobu thought that he had lost. Still he was happy to be one of the finalists. He had been able to play two concertos with an orchestra. He was not the winner, but he was still happy.

Then something amazing happened. Nobu's name was called. There were two first-prize winners! Both Nobu and the Chinese pianist received gold medals. Van Cliburn embraced Nobu. There were tears in Nobu's eyes. They were tears of thanks for the help and support of his family, teachers, and friends. Nobu could not see them, but he said, "I can see them with the eyes of my heart."

[Part 4]

Nobu wants to share the beauty and joy of music with others. He was moved by the Great East Japan Earthquake and wrote an elegy for the victims. He first played it in Boulder, Colorado, on March 31, 2011. He plays it when people ask for an encore. He also played a piano that survived the tsunami. It was washed away and later found and repaired.

Nobu says, "I believe in the power of music. Everybody understands the language of music. What I would like to do is to tell people never to give up. Perhaps my music can help them feel at least a little stronger."

Nobu and some Fukushima junior high school students recorded "Hana wa Saku." It is a charity song for the disaster victims. The students had seen so much suffering. The pianist was able to see their suffering with the eyes of his heart. They joined together in a song to express their sorrow, their courage, and their hope for the future.

〈評価発問の例〉

PART 1

What kind of music do you like? Why?

PART 2

What kind of event was the most memorable in your life?

PART 3

What kind of prize have you ever gotten?

PART 4

Can you give any examples of the power of music?

〈*CROWN English Communication I New Edition*（三省堂，平成 29 年度発行）の LESSON 6　Roots & Shoots に関する評価発問の例〉（※本文は 4.4 を参照）

PART 1

How should you prepare yourself in order to pass a university entrance exam?

PART 2

What do other people say about your character?
Do you agree with them? Why? Why not?

PART 3

We humans are in danger of destroying our environment.
What are some ways to avoid destroying our environment as individuals?

PART 4

What kind of change would you like to make for your future?

評価発問に対する自分の答えをリテリングに取り入れるとより独自性の高いリテリングになります。

## 6.6.2　レッスン終了後に発展的な活動をする

レッスン終了後に行う本文に関連するプロジェクト型の活動を紹介します。図6-2は，*CROWN English Communication I New Edition*（三省堂，平成29年度発行）の LESSON 1 When Words Won't Work が終了した後に，"Make your own Pictogram" という活動を行ったときの生徒の作品です。これはオリジナルのピクトグラムを書かせ，それを英語で説明する活動です。ペアやグループで発表もさせます。評価のためのルーブリックは事前に提示します（※本文は4.2を参照）。

オリジナルのピクトグラムを作ろう！

Class( ) Number( ) Name( )

This pictogram means that we must not sleep during in class.
I think this is very important.
Sometimes we will become sleepy during in class.
But we must not sleep.
We have need to listen to teachers story.
If this pictogram is in my classroom, I can take a class more hard.
So I think I want to realize this pictogram.
Why don't you take a class with this pictogram.

|  | 5点 | 3点 | 1点 |
|---|---|---|---|
| Originality | Excellent | Good | Difficult to understand |
| Content | Explained well | Understandable, but needs some improvement | Needs a lot of improvement |
| Amount | Excellent | Enough | Not enough |

図6-2　"Make your own Pictogram" の作品例

図 6-3 は，*CROWN English Communication I New Edition*（三省堂，平成29 年度発行）の LESSON 5　Food Bank を題材として，"Make your own NPO" という活動を行ったときの生徒の作品です。これは，ペアでオリジナルの NPO を考えさせ，その NPO の名前，ロゴ，世界のどんな問題を解決しようとしているのか，その問題をどのように解決するのかを英語で書かせて，発表させる活動です（本文は 6.5.1 を参照）。

### Lesson 5: Food Bank – Make Your Own NPO

An NPO is a non-profit organization. That means they need the support of other people, companies, and the government to help make the world a better place. There are many kinds of NPOs in the world. In the boxes below, create your own NPO and answer the questions. Your NPO can help any big or small problem in the world! Remember: more creative or original, the better! You can create funny NPOs too!

| Name of your organization | Logo |
|---|---|
| Protect Green! | tree, leaves |

**What problem in the world are you trying to solve?**

Green is lost now all over the world. Because popole destroy trees and burn glasslands.

A lot of problems will arise if plants are gone as it is. For example, when plants and trees fall the animal's lives and food are gone. Also the supply of oxygen will go away, and someday many creatures will die. Even humans can not live.

Therefore, it is necessary to ban the suppression of more trees and to plant trees or plants in spaces where there are no them.

**How will your NPO try to solve it?**

First, makes the law, to stop people from cutting trees.
Second, plants trees or plants in spaces where there are no them. Also, do activities to get more people to know about this work.

In addition, we teach people the importance of trees and plants. I think that this is the most important activity. If this importance spreads all over the world, these problems will be solved.

図6-3　"Make your own NPO" の作品例

## 6.6.3 本文の内容に関連するディスカッションを行う

　レッスン終了後に，そのレッスンに関連するディスカッショントピック
を与えて，ペアやグループでディスカッションをさせる活動です。どのよ
うなディスカッショントピックを設定するのがよいのかを考えるときには，
まずは，そのレッスンのねらいを明確にするのがよいでしょう。そのレッ
スン内容に基づいて，生徒たちにどのような変容を求めたいのかを考えて
ください。レッスンのねらいとディスカッショントピックを深く関連付け
ることで，本文の内容理解を超えた意味のあるディスカッションをさせる
ことができます。以下は，*CROWN English Communication I New Edition*
（三省堂，平成29年度発行）の Lesson 6　Roots & Shoots におけるディス
カッション例です。また，Lesson 6 以外のレッスンのねらいとそのねら
いに関連したディスカッショントピック例も紹介します。

Lesson 6
| タイトル |
Roots & Shoots
| 学習のねらい |
　動物学者・環境保護活動家であるジェーン・グドールのインタビューを
通して彼女が行う環境保護活動について学ばせるとともに，人と動物との
共生や環境問題について考えさせる。
| ディスカッショントピック |
We humans are in danger of destroying our environment.
What are some ways to avoid destroying our environment as individuals?

| ディスカッション例 |
A：What are some ways to avoid destroying our environment as individuals?
　　Do you have any ideas?
B：I think that we should reduce our waste at home. Especially, much of our
　　waste at home comes from foods. So, we should buy only a necessary
　　amount of food.

C：Many people go to work by car. It produces a lot of harmful gas. If possible, they should go to work on foot or by bike.

D：We should recycle old products and separate our waste properly.

Lesson 1

タイトル

When Words Won't Work

学習のねらい

　ピクトグラムの有用性を理解し，ピクトグラムを言語と比較することで，ピクトグラムが持つメッセージの効果について考えさせるとともに，身の回りにあるピクトグラムについて考えさせる。

ディスカッショントピック

What kind of pictogram do you see in your daily life?

Lesson 2

タイトル

Going into Space

学習のねらい

　宇宙飛行士である若田光一さんの話を通して，職業観について考えさせるとともに，将来，自分はどのようなことに対して人生を捧げたいと思うのかについて考えさせる。

ディスカッショントピック

What is your dream?

Lesson 3

タイトル

A Canoe Is an Island

学習のねらい

　ホクレア号で航海を行った内野加奈子さんの話を通して，自然とともに生きるとはどのようなことであるのかについて考えさせるとともに，自分

は何に対して感謝の気持ちを抱いているのかについて考えさせる。

ディスカッショントピック

Who or what do you have a deep appreciation for?


Lesson 4

タイトル

Seeing with the Eyes of the Heart

学習のねらい

　ピアニストである辻井伸行さんが困難を乗り越えて，偉業を成し遂げるという話を通して，いかなる逆境に置かれようとも，あきらめずに目標に向かって努力する大切さについて考えさせる。

ディスカッショントピック

What do you think is one of the keys to success in life? And why?


Lesson 5

タイトル

Food Bank

学習のねらい

　フードバンクの目的や活動内容について知り，社会的な問題を解決しようとする態度を育てるとともに，社会問題を解決するためにどのようなNPO の設立が考えられるのかについて考えさせる。

ディスカッショントピック

If you set up your own NPO, what kind of NPO would it be?


Lesson 7

タイトル

Paper Architect

学習のねらい

　紙管を使って被災地で支援を行う建築家である坂茂さんの活動を通して，強い信念を持ち続けることの大切さを学ばせるとともに，これまでの人生

で最も印象に残っている出来事について振り返らせ，その出来事から自分が学んだことについて考えさせる。

ディスカッショントピック

What kind of event was the most memorable in your life?

Lesson 8

タイトル

Not So Long Ago

学習のねらい

　20世紀を代表するいくつかの写真が持つメッセージを感じ取り，人間が過去に犯した過ちについて考えさせるとともに，みんなが笑顔で暮らすことのできる明るい未来を構築するためには何が必要であるのかについて考えさせる。

ディスカッショントピック

What kind of message would you like to give to people in the next generation?

Lesson 9

タイトル

Crossing the "Uncanny Valley"

学習のねらい

　アンドロイドロボットを研究する研究者である石黒浩さんの話を通して，人とロボットが共生する未来について考えさせる。

ディスカッショントピック

Do you want to have the future when you will live with an android? And why?

Lesson 10

タイトル

Good Ol'Charlie Brown

学習のねらい

　漫画『ピーナッツ』の登場人物の言葉や行動から，「本当の強さとは？」や「人を思いやるとは？」といった人生哲学について考えさせる。

ディスカッショントピック

Which Peanuts characters do you like best? And why?

## 第6章のまとめ

〈リテリングの手順〉
- （Ⅰ）内容理解
- （Ⅱ）音読による内在化
- （Ⅲ）発話情報の選定
- （Ⅳ）英語への変換
- （Ⅴ）**発話**

● リテリングの方法には，「口頭によるもの」と，「筆記によるもの」がある。口頭によるものは，スピーキング力の育成をねらいとし，筆記によるものはライティング力の育成をねらいとしている。

● リテリングデータの収集方法として，口頭によるリテリングデータはICレコーダーで録音ができ，筆記によるリテリングデータは紙に書くことで記録できる。それらのデータは，リテリングの質や量に対する振り返りや，誤りの発見や修正に利用できる。

● リテリングにおける技能統合については，「読んで→話す」，「読んで→書く」，「聞いて→話す」，「聞いて→書く」という4つの種類があり，指導のねらいに応じて使い分ける。

● リテリングを行うときの形態には，「個人」，「ペア」，「グループ」，「全体発表」という4つの種類があり，心理的な負荷を考慮しながら，自信を持って，他の生徒にリテリングできるように，段階的に指導をするように心がける。

● ペアやグループによるリテリング①：1人1文リテリング

1人ひとりが，同じ手がかりを見ながら1文ずつ順番にリテリングをする。

　［利点］

　　1人ずつ順番に担当するので，責任感が生まれ，主体性が高まる。

●ペアやグループによるリテリング②：繰り返しリテリング

　1人ひとりが，同じ手がかりを見ながら1文ずつ順番にリテリングをし，自分の順番より前に話された内容についても，再度話してから，続きの1文を話す。

　［利点］

　　全員が同じ手がかりを用いてリテリングをするので，多様なリテリングを聞くことができ，他の生徒のパラフレーズから学ぶことができる。

●ペアやグループによるリテリング③：ジグソーリテリング

　「ホームグループ」と「エキスパートグループ」を使い分けて，1人に1パートを割り当てて行うリテリングである。

　［利点］

　　役割分担があることで責任感を持ち，より自主的にリテリングに取り組む傾向がある。また，インフォメーションギャップがあることで，他の生徒のリテリングを主体的に聞いたり，インタラクションが生まれたりする。

●既習レッスンを用いて，帯活動としてリテリングを行う場合には，「英語の授業に臨む動機を高めることができる」，「スピーキングの機会を増やすことができる」，「既習レッスンの復習を行うことができる」といった利点がある。

●リテリングを高度化するためのアイデアとして，「本文に関する自分の意見を追加する」，「登場人物の気持ちを推測して追加する」，「本文の続きを推測して追加する」，「ダイアローグ・リテリングを行う」，「プレゼンテーション・リテリングを行う」といったアイデアがあり，生徒の英語習熟度や指導のねらいに応じて，学期に1回

ぐらいの頻度でもよいのでトライさせるとよい。

●アウトプットⅢの活動として,「本文の内容に関連する評価発問を
する」,「レッスン終了後に発展的な活動をする」,「本文の内容に関
連するディスカッションを行う」といったものがあり, 毎レッスン
のゴールをアウトプットⅡであるリテリングに留めずに, 即興型の
自己表現活動であるアウトプットⅢを定期的に取り入れてトライさ
せるとよい。

## 第7章

# どのようにリテリングを評価するのか

　リテリングを取り入れた授業を行うときには，授業と評価の一体化という観点からもリテリングに対する評価を行うべきです。評価といっても，成績に影響するものもあれば，振り返りとして使用し，次のリテリングに繋げるための評価もあります。ここでは，様々なリテリングの評価について考えます。

## 7.1　パフォーマンステストとしての評価

　パフォーマンステストとしてリテリングを行うときに考慮するべき点として，まずリテリングの範囲があります。1課全体に対してリテリングをさせるのか，パートを指定してリテリングをさせるのかを考えなければなりません。また，手がかりを事前に提示しておくのか，あるいは，パフォーマンステストの直前に提示するのかも検討する必要があります。既習レッスンを用いたリテリングのパフォーマンステストの場合には，テスト前に準備をすることが可能なので即興的なリテリングとはなりません。即興的なリテリングをさせたいのであれば，使用している検定教科書の内容と関連する題材を扱った別のテキストをその場で初見で読ませてから，リテリングをさせるのがよいでしょう。40人学級で1人ずつ評価をする場合には，1人5分かかったとしても約200分の時間が必要となるので，ICレコーダーやiPadを利用し，一斉に録音をさせて，後で評価をするのがよいでしょう。評価をするためのツールとして，ルーブリックを使用します。ルーブリックとは，学習の達成度を表を用いて測定する評価方法のことです。クラスごとの評価の公平性を保つためにも，事前に担当者同士

でルーブリックを用いた評価トレーニングが必要です。ルーブリックによる評価方法について，小泉（2016）では，以下の2種類を紹介しています。

（ア）総合的評価（holistic）
　　　○発話を全体的に評価する。
　　　○1つの得点を出す。
（イ）分析的評価（analytic）
　　　○発音，流暢さなどの評価項目ごとに評価する。
　　　○複数の得点を出す。

　リテリングにおける総合的評価を用いたルーブリックの例としては，卯城（2009）で紹介している表7-1のルーブリックがあります。このルーブリックでは，リテリングのパフォーマンスを総合的に評価し，1回のリテ

| レベル | 評価基準 |
|---|---|
| 5 | テキスト原文の再生にとどまることなく，内容を概括することができている。リテリングに主題や要点，適切な細部情報を含むことができている。リテリングには十分な一貫性があり，完成度が高い。 |
| 4 | リテリングに主題や要点，適切な細部情報を含むことができている。リテリングには十分な一貫性がある。 |
| 3 | 要点を関連づけることができている。リテリングには適切な細部情報を含むことができており，適度な一貫性がある。 |
| 2 | いくつかの要点を関連づけることができている。リテリングには適切な細部情報を含むことができており，ある程度の一貫性がある。全体的に理解可能な内容である。 |
| 1 | 細部情報だけを関連づけている。一貫性はまったくなく，不完全である。 |

※筆者によって一部改変しています。

表7-1　総合的評価の例（Irwin & Mitchell, 1983）

リングに対して，1つの得点を与えるので，総合的なリテリングの評価を示すことができます。

　リテリングにおける分析的評価を用いたルーブリックとしては，表7-2のようにいくつかの評価項目を設定し，それぞれの評価項目に対して得点を与えていくので，どの項目ができて，どの項目ができていなかったのかを示すことができます。また，AET に協力をしてもらえるならば，例えば，発音，流暢さ，パラフレーズの評価を AET が担当し，アイコンタクトと内容についての評価を日本人英語教師が担当するなどして，2人で協力して評価をすることもできます。文法的な正確さも評価項目に入れることは可能ですが，基本的に，話す量が増えれば増えるほど，誤りの数が多くなる傾向があるので，たくさん発話させたいのであれば，評価項目として使用しなくてもよいでしょう。

| 評価項目 | 5点 | 3点 | 1点 |
|---|---|---|---|
| 発音<br>（Pronunciation） | ほとんどの語を正確に発音している。 | おおむね良いが，発音の誤りがいくつかある。 | 正確に発音していない語が多い。 |
| 流暢さ<br>（Fluency） | 流暢に話している。 | 発話速度はやや遅めである。 | 発話速度が遅い。 |
| アイコンタクト<br>（Eye contact） | ほぼ最初から最後まで聴き手の顔を見ながら話している。 | 半分以上の時間は聴き手の顔を見ながら話している。 | 聴き手の顔をほとんど見ずに話している。 |
| 内容<br>（Contents） | 指定された手がかりをすべて使用して本文の内容を正確に伝えている。 | 指定された手がかりをいくつか使用して本文の内容をある程度伝えている。 | 指定された手がかりをほとんど使用せず，本文の内容を伝えていない。 |
| パラフレーズ<br>（Paraphrase） | 原文とは異なる言語形式を多く使用している。 | 原文とは異なる言語形式をいくつか使用している。 | 原文とは異なる言語形式をほとんど使用していない。 |

表7-2　分析的評価

表7-2 にある評価項目以外の項目を追加することはできますが，生徒の
パフォーマンスを聞きながら多くの項目を評価するのは難しいので，評価
項目を増やす場合には，生徒のパフォーマンスをiPadやビデオカメラ等
で録画して，後で時間のあるときに評価するのが現実的でしょう。表7-2
にある評価項目以外の項目例を表7-3 に記載します。

| 評価項目 | 5点 | 3点 | 1点 |
|---|---|---|---|
| 要点 | 要点をすべて入れて，内容を伝えている。 | 要点をほぼ入れて，内容を伝えている。 | 要点が少なく，内容を伝えきれていない。 |
| 細部情報 | 細部情報をすべて入れて，内容を伝えている。 | 細部情報をほぼ入れて，内容を伝えている。 | 細部情報が少ない。 |
| 本文に関する自分の意見（質） | 本文に関する自分の意見が明確で理解しやすい。 | 本文に関する自分の意見が一部理解しにくい。 | 本文に関する自分の意見が理解しにくい。 |
| 本文に関する自分の意見（量） | 本文に関する自分の意見が多い。 | 本文に関する自分の意見がやや少ない。 | 本文に関する自分の意見が少なすぎる。 |
| 即興質問への応答 | リテリングをした内容に関する即興質問に適切に応答している。 | リテリングをした内容に関する即興質問にほぼ適切に応答している。 | リテリングをした内容に関する即興質問に適切に応答していない。 |

表7-3　その他の評価項目の例

## 7.2　ペアやグループによる評価

　ペアやグループの形態で生徒同士によってリテリングを評価させるとき
には，教師が有するような評価能力を必要とせずに生徒同士で容易に評価
することができる以下のような評価表を使用するのがよいでしょう。ここ
では，*Revised LANDMARK English Communication I*（啓林館，平成29年度

発行）の LESSON 10　Friendship over Time における評価表を紹介します
（※本文は 4.1 を参照）。

　表 7-4 は本文に関する内容について評価をすることができます。リスト
アップされている本文に関する情報についてパートナーが発話することが
できたら，チェック欄に○を記入します。本文中のどの情報を発話するこ
とができ，どの情報を発話することができなかったのかを確認することが
できます。

| LESSON 10　Part 1 | チェック欄 |
|---|---|
| ■　イラクの突然の発表 | |
| ■　イランにいた外国人の行動 | |
| ■　イランと日本の定期便のこと | |
| ■　イランの日本大使館の行動 | |
| ■　外国の航空会社の対応 | |
| ■　200 人を超える日本人の状況 | |
| ■　日本大使館が受け取った電話の内容 | |
| ■　イランの日本人救出 | |
| ■　日本のマスコミの報道 | |
| ■　トルコが日本人を救ってくれた本当の理由 | |

表7-4　ペアによるリテリングの評価表①

　表 7-5 は，キーワードの使用について評価をすることができます。パー
トナーがリストアップされているキーワードを使用することができたら，
チェック欄に○を記入します。どのキーワードを使用することができ，ど
のキーワードを使用することができなかったのかを確認することができま
す。

| | キーワード | チェック欄 | | キーワード | チェック欄 |
|---|---|---|---|---|---|
| 1 | shoot | | 6 | 200 | |
| 2 | hurry | | 7 | special | |
| 3 | regular | | 8 | helped | |
| 4 | embassy | | 9 | top | |
| 5 | priority | | 10 | risk | |

表7-5　ペアによるリテリングの評価表②

## 7.3　個人による振り返り

　リテリングの後には，自分のパフォーマンスについて記述形式で振り返りをさせることで，自分のできた部分とできなかった部分を検証させるのがよいでしょう。自己評価をすることは，リテリング技術の向上につながります。振り返りのための項目については，様々な項目が考えられます。次ページの表7-6は振り返りシートの例です。

## 7.4　評価に競争意識を取り入れてリテリングを活性化させる

　ペアやグループでのリテリングに競争意識を取り入れ，リテリングを活性化させることができます。ビジネスの世界には「ゲーミフィケーション」という言葉があり，これは，人を夢中にさせるゲーム作りのノウハウをゲーム以外の分野に応用して，楽しみながら取り組む仕掛けを作り出すことを意味します。語彙学習アプリで語彙問題を解きながら高得点を目指していくようなものも「ゲーミフィケーション」の一種です。リテリングの中に「ゲーミフィケーション」を取り入れるアイデアを紹介します。

### 7.4.1　語数における競い合い

　ペアやグループでリテリングをするときに，ある一定時間内にどれだけの語数を発話したのかという観点で競い合わせることができます。この競い合いでは，西（2010）にある「ワードカウンター」を使用します（124ページの表7-7参照）。「ワードカウンター」とは，指で発話語数を数える

| 時間内に言えたのか？　言えなかった原因は何か？ |
|---|
| |
| 要点を整理して言えたのか？　言えなかったなら，その原因は何か？ |
| |
| パラフレーズはできたのか？　できなかったなら，その原因は何か？ |
| |
| 使用できなかった語彙・表現はあるか？ |
| |
| 次回のリテリングに向けて意識して取り組むべきこと |
| |

表7-6　リテリング振り返りシートの例

ツールです。例えば，ペアによるリテリングの場合には，Aがリテリングしているときに，Bが「ワードカウンター」に指を置き，書かれている数字の上に指を沿わせて，Aの発話語数を数えます。

　また，「ワードカウンター記録用紙」を作成することで，リテリングを複数回行ったときの総語数を記録することができるので，リテリングの上達度を可視化できます。「ワードカウンター」はリテリングだけでなく，記録用紙内の4にあるように「制服に賛成か反対か」といったような即興的スピーキング活動にも「ワードカウンター」を使用することができます。

## 7.4.2　本文内容とキーワード使用における競い合い

　これは，7.2で紹介した表7-4, 7-5に配点欄を追加して，ペアで合計得点を競い合わせるものです。次ページの表7-8は，情報の重要度に応じて配点を記載し，125ページの表7-9は，使えるようになってほしい語彙の

| 1 | 50 | 51 | 100 | 101 | 150 | 151 | 200 |
|---|---|---|---|---|---|---|---|
| 2 | 49 | 52 | 99 | 102 | 149 | 152 | 199 |
| … | … | … | … | … | … | … | … |
| 24 | 27 | 74 | 77 | 124 | 127 | 174 | 177 |
| 25 | 26 | 75 | 76 | 125 | 126 | 175 | 176 |

|  | 日付 | LESSON / Part | 1回目 | 2回目 | 3回目 | 4回目 | 5回目 |
|---|---|---|---|---|---|---|---|
| 1 | 4 /24 | L2 / P1 | 32 | 45 | 65 | 70 | 75 |
| 2 | 4 /29 | L2 / P2 | 24 | 28 | 35 | 41 | 53 |
| 3 | 5 / 8 | L2 / P3 | 41 | 47 | 53 | 58 | 64 |
| 4 | 5 /15 | 制服に<br>賛成 or 反対 | 15 | 27 | 42 |  |  |
| 5 |  |  |  |  |  |  |  |

表7-7　ワードカウンターとワードカウンターの記録用紙の例

| LESSON 10 Part 1 | 配点 | 得点 |
|---|---|---|
| ■　イラクの突然の発表 | 2点 |  |
| ■　イランにいた外国人の行動 | 1点 |  |
| ■　イランと日本の定期便のこと | 1点 |  |
| ■　イランの日本大使館の行動 | 1点 |  |
| ■　外国の航空会社の対応 | 2点 |  |
| ■　200人を超える日本人の状況 | 1点 |  |
| ■　日本大使館が受け取った電話の内容 | 2点 |  |
| ■　イランの日本人救出 | 1点 |  |
| ■　日本のマスコミの報道 | 1点 |  |
| ■　トルコが日本人を救ってくれた本当の理由 | 2点 |  |
| 合　計 | 14点中 |  |

表7-8　本文内容における競い合い

| キーワード | 配点 | 得点 | キーワード | 配点 | 得点 |
|---|---|---|---|---|---|
| 1　shoot | 1 点 | | 6　200 | 1 点 | |
| 2　hurry | 1 点 | | 7　special | 2 点 | |
| 3　regular | 2 点 | | 8　helped | 2 点 | |
| 4　embassy | 1 点 | | 9　top | 1 点 | |
| 5　priority | 2 点 | | 10　risk | 2 点 | |
| 合　計 | 15 点中 | | （　　　）点 | | |

表7-9　キーワード使用における競い合い

観点から配点を記載しました。

　また，表7-10のように，対戦相手や勝敗の記入欄を追加するのもよい
でしょう。

| 日付 | LESSON / Part | 対戦相手 | 勝敗 |
|---|---|---|---|
| 6 /12 | L4 / P1 | 吉田君 | ○ |
| 6 /17 | L4 / P2 | 中川さん | × |
| 6 /22 | L4 / P3 | 田中君 | △ |
| | | | |

表7-10　勝敗表

## 7.5　定期考査に，リテリングに関連した問題を出題しよう

　授業でリテリングを継続して行うならば，授業と評価の一体化という観
点からも，定期考査の問題にリテリングに関連した問題を取り入れたいも
のです。リテリングをやればやるほど，定期考査で高得点を取ることがで
きると実感できれば，授業内や家庭での取り組み状況も良くなるでしょう。
以下は，靜（2002）を参考にして，*LANDMARK English Communication I*
（啓林館，平成25年度発行）の LESSON 6　The Doctor with the Hands of

God の Part 4 を題材とした定期考査の問題例を 7.5.1〜7.5.6 で紹介します。

LESSON 6  The Doctor with the Hands of God
[Part 4]

Today, as an experienced surgeon, Dr. Fukushima teaches his methods to students and younger doctors. One time, during an operation, a younger doctor made a mistake. As soon as Dr. Fukushima noticed it, he took the surgical knife away from the doctor. He then went on lecturing the doctor for six hours while he was correcting the mistake. When he sees younger doctors working too slowly, he always teaches them to work more quickly and carefully. He is a strict teacher but the younger doctors respect him very much. They know that the patient is always his top priority.

## 7.5.1　削除された語の位置を指摘する：リプロダクションレベル

英文には，（ア）〜（オ）の語が削除されています。それぞれの語が本来どこにあったのか指摘しなさい。本来あった位置に戻した場合に，その前と後に来る語を書くこと。

| （ア）experienced　（イ）it　（ウ）on　（エ）working　（オ）strict |
| --- |

Today, as an surgeon, Dr. Fukushima teaches his methods to students and younger doctors. One time, during an operation, a younger doctor made a mistake. As soon as Dr. Fukushima noticed, he took the surgical knife away from the doctor. He then went lecturing the doctor for six hours while he was correcting the mistake. When he sees younger doctors too slowly, he always teaches them to work more quickly and carefully. He is a teacher but the younger doctors respect him very much. They know that the patient is always his top priority.

[解答]
（ア）an / surgeon　（イ）noticed / he　（ウ）went / lecturing

126

（エ）doctors / too　（オ）a / teacher

## 7.5.2　内容的・文法的な誤りを訂正する：リプロダクションレ ベル

英文には，内容的あるいは文法的な誤りが5か所あります。（ア）誤っ ている箇所を指摘し，（イ）誤りのないように訂正しなさい。

Today, as an experienced surgeon, Dr. Fukushima teaches his methods for students and younger doctors. One time, while an operation, a younger doctor made a mistake. As soon as Dr. Fukushima noticed it, he took the surgical knife away from the doctor. He then went on lecturing the doctor for six hours while he was collecting the mistake. When he sees younger doctors worked too slowly, he always teaches them to work more quickly and carefully. He is a kind teacher but the younger doctors respect him very much. They know that the patient is always his top priority.

［解答］
for → to / while → during / collecting → correcting
worked → working / kind → strict

## 7.5.3　英文中の語と定義のマッチング：リテリングレベル

以下の（ア）～（ウ）の意味で使われている語を，英文から抜き出しなさ い。

（ア）something that has been done in the wrong way
（イ）expecting people to obey rules or to do what you say
（ウ）the thing that you think is most important

Today, as an experienced surgeon, Dr. Fukushima teaches his methods to students and younger doctors. One time, during an operation, a younger doctor made a mistake. As soon as Dr. Fukushima noticed it, he took the surgical knife away from the doctor. He then went on lecturing the doctor for six hours while he was correcting the mistake. When he sees younger doctors working too slowly, he always teaches them to work more quickly and carefully. He is a strict teacher but the younger doctors respect him very much. They know that the patient is always his top priority.

［解答］
（ア）mistake　（イ）strict　（ウ）priority

## 7.5.4　パラフレーズされた本文の空所を補充する：リテリング　レベル
［A］とほぼ同様の内容を別の表現で言い換えたものが［B］である。
（　　）に入る語を答えなさい。語頭の文字は与えられています。

［A］
　Today, as an experienced surgeon, Dr. Fukushima teaches his methods to students and younger doctors. One time, during an operation, a younger doctor made a mistake. As soon as Dr. Fukushima noticed it, he took the surgical knife away from the doctor. He then went on lecturing the doctor for six hours while he was correcting the mistake. When he sees younger doctors working too slowly, he always teaches them to work more quickly and carefully. He is a strict teacher but the younger doctors respect him very much. They know that the patient is always his top priority.

［B］
　Today, as a surgeon with much（1）(e　　　）, Dr. Fukushima teaches students and younger doctors his（2）(w　　　）of operating. One time, when they were doing an operation, a younger doctor made a mistake. When Dr. Fukushima noticed the（3）(m　　　）, he took away the doctor's surgical knife. Then he（4）(c　　　）to lecture the doctor for six hours while he was correcting the mistake. If he sees that younger doctors are working

too slowly, he always shows them（5）(h　　　) to work faster and with greater（6）(c　　　). Dr. Fukushima is a strict teacher but the younger doctors have great（7）(r　　　) for him. They know that the patient is always the most（8）(i　　　) person for him.

［解答］
（1）experience　（2）ways　（3）mistake　（4）continued
（5）how　（6）care　（7）respect　（8）important

　また，語を書かせるだけでなく，以下のように語句を書かせることもできます。

　Today, as a surgeon（1）＿＿＿＿＿＿＿＿, Dr. Fukushima teaches students and younger doctors（2）＿＿＿＿＿＿＿＿. One time, when they were doing an operation, a younger doctor made a mistake. When Dr. Fukushima noticed the mistake, he took away the doctor's surgical knife. Then he（3）＿＿＿＿＿＿＿＿ the doctor for six hours while he was correcting the mistake. If he sees that younger doctors are working too slowly, he always（4）＿＿＿＿＿＿＿＿ to work faster and（5）＿＿＿＿＿＿＿＿. Dr. Fukushima is a strict teacher but the younger doctors have great respect for him. They know that the patient is always（6）＿＿＿＿＿＿＿＿ for him.

## 7.5.5　要約をする：リテリングレベル

　授業で読んだ "LESSON 6 The Doctor with the Hands of God" の内容を150 語〜200 語の英語で要約しなさい。
　　→このタイプの問題を出題する場合には，出題を予告しておくのがよいでしょう。また，「自分の言葉を多く使用している」のような評価項目を記載したルーブリックを事前に配布すると，より質の高い要約を書かせることができます。

## 7.5.6　自己表現をする：自己表現レベル

　授業では，"LESSON 6 The Doctor with the Hands of God" を読み，福島先生のモットーを学びました。あなたは，医者が持つべき最も重要な資質は何であると考えますか。理由とともに，150～200 語程度の英語で書きなさい。

　　→定期考査では時間の制約があるので，このタイプの問題を出題する場合にも事前に予告しておくのがよいでしょう。評価をするときには，表 7-11 のようなルーブリックを使用するとよいでしょう。

| 評価項目 | | 得点 |
|---|---|---|
| 意見 | 意見があるかどうか | 1 点 |
| 理由 | 意見に対する 2 つの理由があるかどうか | 2 点 |
| | 2 つの理由が意見をサポートしているかどうか | 2 点 |
| 結論 | 結論があるかどうか | 1 点 |
| | 結論が意見とは異なる表現で書かれているかどうか | 1 点 |
| 語数 | 必要語数を満たしているかどうか | 満たしていない<br>→1 点減点 |
| 正確さ | 深刻な文法の誤りや語法の誤りがあるかどうか | 深刻な誤りが多い<br>→2 点減点<br>深刻な誤りが少しある<br>→1 点減点 |
| | | 合計 7 点 |

**表7-11　ルーブリックの例**

## 第7章のまとめ

● リテリングをパフォーマンステストとして行う場合，時間の制約があるので，IC レコーダーや iPad を利用し，一斉に録音をさせて，後で評価をするのがよい。

● リテリングを評価するために，ルーブリックを使用する。ルーブリックには「総合的なルーブリック」と「分析的なルーブリック」があり，前者は，発話を全体的に評価し，1つの得点を与える。後者は，発話を評価項目ごとに評価し，複数の得点を与える。

● ペアやグループにおいて生徒同士でリテリングを評価するときには，本文に関する特定のある内容について話すことができるかどうかをチェックする評価表や，指定されたキーワードを使用することができるかどうかをチェックする評価表がある。

● リテリングの後には，可能な限り記述形式で振り返りをさせることで，できたこととできなかったことを検証でき，リテリング技術の向上につながる。

● リテリングに競争意識を取り入れるアイデアとして，「語数における競い合い」や「内容と語彙使用における競い合い」といったものがあり，競争をさせることでリテリングの活性化が期待できる。

● 授業と評価の一体化の観点からも，定期考査にリテリングに関連した問題を出題するのがよい。

# リテリング研究から分かること

この章では，筆者によるリテリングに関する研究を紹介して，そこから
リテリングに生かせることや，リテリングが学習者にどのような影響を及
ぼすのかなどについて考えます。

## 8.1　リテリングを長期間行った情意面の変化についての研究

第二言語習得において，学習動機の果たす役割が大きいのは言うまでも
ありません。「自己決定理論（Self-Determination Theory）」では，学習動機
が高まる条件として，「自律性（autonomy）」，「有能性（competence）」，「関
係性（relatedness）」があり，主体的に学ぼうとする「自律性」，学習の中
で「できた」という「有能性」，自分1人ではなく，他の生徒と共に学ぶ
という「関係性」の3つの条件が整ったときに学習動機が高まるとされて
います（Ryan, R.M., & Deci, E.L. 2002）。

リテリングを行うときにも，「自己決定理論」の条件を整えることがで
きます。例えば，キーワードの選択を生徒にさせることで「自律性」を高
め，負荷の高い活動であるリテリングを行うことができたという感情は
「有能性」を高め，ペアやグループでリテリングを行うことで「関係性」
を生み出せます。ここでは，一定期間行ったリテリングが生徒の情意面に
どのような変化をもたらしたのかを紹介します。授業では，準備練習とし
ての個人によるリテリングの後に，ペアによるリテリングを行いました。
質問紙は，各質問項目を「自己決定理論」に関連させた加藤（2012）の質
問紙を参考にして7段階のリッカート尺度［1：まったく違う / 2：違
う / 3：やや違う / 4：どちらでもない / 5：ややその通り / 6：その

通り／7：まったくその通り］による質問紙を作成しました。2学期の始まりにあたる8月後半から各パートあるいはレッスン全体のリテリングを行ったので，質問紙による調査は，9月，12月，3月の3回実施しました。

　この研究によって，一定期間，リテリングを行うことで，リテリングに対する動機が上昇したことが確認され，リテリングが生徒の情意面に肯定的な影響を及ぼすことが示唆されました。協力者は公立高校1年生1クラス（38名）です。調査結果は表8-1を見てください。

| 質問項目 | 9月 M (SD) | 12月 M (SD) | 3月 M (SD) |
|---|---|---|---|
| 1　リテリングを集中してできる。 | 4.4 (1.1) | 5.1 (1.0) | 5.3 (1.2) |
| 2　リテリングに熱心に取り組んでいる。 | 4.7 (1.1) | 5.0 (1.1) | 5.1 (1.0) |
| 3　リテリングをおもしろいと思う。 | 3.7 (1.4) | 4.2 (1.4) | 4.6 (1.3) |
| 4　リテリングを楽しみにしている。 | 3.0 (1.2) | 3.6 (1.3) | 3.7 (1.3) |
| 5　リテリングでは自分から進んで参加しようと思う。 | 3.4 (1.1) | 3.8 (1.2) | 4.2 (1.3) |
| 6　リテリングでは「できた」という充実感が得られる。 | 4.8 (1.4) | 4.8 (1.3) | 5.3 (1.3) |
| 7　リテリングではペアやグループで教え合いながらできる。 | 4.0 (0.9) | 4.2 (0.7) | 4.8 (1.0) |

表8-1　質問紙による調査結果

　統計分析の結果，9月と3月の平均の差において，質問項目1，3，7は効果量が大，質問項目2，4，5，6は効果量が中でした（効果量とは，あ

る実験の効果を見るための指標です）。一定期間，リテリングを行うことで，リテリングに対する動機が上昇したことが確認され，リテリングが生徒の情意面に肯定的な影響を及ぼすことが示唆されました。

## 8.2 IC レコーダーを活用したスピーキング研究

本研究は，2018年度のパナソニック教育財団実践研究助成を受けた研究であり，普通教室において，IC レコーダーを活用して，一定期間リテリングを行うことで，生徒のスピーキング力が高まるのかについて，「流暢さ」に焦点を当てて検証した研究です。また，スピーキングに対する情意面がどのように変化するのかを質問紙調査で検証しました。この研究の結果から，IC レコーダーを活用すると，スピーキングにおける「流暢さ」が高まることと，スピーキングに対する情意面に肯定的な影響を及ぼすことが示唆されました。協力者は，公立高校の１年生２クラス（80名）です。

### 8.2.1 研究の過程

表8-2は研究の経過を示したものです。

「スピーキング課題」は，英検２級２次試験の過去問題を使用しました。３コマの絵を口頭で描写するものです。30秒間の準備後に，40秒間の発話を録音しました。

「スピーキングに対する情意面の調査」は，8.1と同様に加藤（2012）の質問紙を参考にして７段階のリカートスケールによる質問紙を使用しました。また，「リテリングについての意見調査」と「IC レコーダーについての意見調査」は自由記述としました。

### 8.2.2 授業展開

本研究の授業展開は，以下の「基本的な授業展開」と「ジグソーリテリング」の２種類に分けられます。

| 時期 | 取り組み内容 | 評価のための記録 |
|---|---|---|
| 6月上旬 | ●スピーキング力の調査（事前）<br>●スピーキングに対する情意面の調査<br>（事前） | ○スピーキング課題<br>○質問紙調査（7件法） |
| 6月中旬 | ICレコーダーの使い方指導 | |
| 7月<br>8月<br>9月<br>10月<br>11月<br>12月<br>1月 | L3　A Canoe Is an Island<br>L4　Seeing with the Eyes of the Heart<br>L5　Food Bank<br>L6　Roots & Shoots<br>L7　Paper Architect<br>L8　Not So Long Ago<br>L9　Crossing the "Uncanny Valley" | *Crown English Communication I New Edition*（三省堂，平成29年度発行）を使用。 |
| 1月下旬 | ●スピーキング力の調査（事後）<br>●スピーキングに対する情意面の調査<br>（事後）<br>●リテリングについての意見調査<br>●ICレコーダーについての意見調査 | ○スピーキング課題<br>○質問紙調査（7件法）<br>○質問紙調査（自由記述）<br>○質問紙調査（自由記述） |

表8-2　研究の経過

**【基本的な授業展開】**　※本研究では，L3，4，5，9で実践

（1）語彙指導——リテリングのために，日本語訳を見て英語が言えるように指導する。

（2）内容理解①——教科書を閉本してICレコーダーにある本文の音声を聞いて，本文の内容に関する質問に答えさせる。次に，教科書を読んで同じ質問に答えさせる。［リスニング→リーディング］

（3）内容理解②——本文にある複雑な構造を持った文などについて解説が記載されたプリントを配布し，必要な解説を行う。

（4）音読——様々な音読法を用いて，発音の強化と言語材料の内在化を行う。

（5）リテリング——パートごとにキーワードを自分で選び，絵や記号なども追加してリテリング用メモを作成させる。その後，そのメモを見ながら，リテリングを行い，ICレコーダーに録音させ，イヤホンを用いて自分の発話を聞いて振り返りを行わせる。これを数回続けた後に，ペアでリテリングを行わせる。また，グループを作り，グループ内の生徒とICレコーダーを交換して他の生徒のリテリングを聞き，良かった点，修正点，改善方法を話し合わ

せる。
（6）即興的なアウトプット活動——本文の内容に関連した評価発問をして，即興的な応答をさせ，それを IC レコーダーに録音させ，振り返りを行わせる。

〈ジグソーリテリング〉　※本研究では，L6，7，8 で実践。

（1）語彙指導——全パートの語彙について日本訳を見て英語が言えるように指導する。
（2）担当パートの割り当て＋内容理解——4 人グループを作り，1 人ひとりに担当パートを割り当て，その担当パートのみ「基本的な授業展開」と同様のやり方で内容理解を行わせる。ただし，教師の解説は行わない。
（3）リテリングの練習（個人）——個人で音読を何度もさせる。その後に，リテリング用メモを作成させて，IC レコーダーにリテリングを数回録音させ，振り返りを行わせ，リテリングの質を高めさせる。
（4）リテリングの練習（グループ）——担当パートが同じ生徒をグループにして，お互いのリテリングの良かった点，修正点，改善方法を話し合わせる。
（5）リテリングの本番——担当パートが異なる生徒をグループにして，本文の内容の順番通りに 1 人ずつリテリングをさせ，自分の担当パート以外では，メモを取りながら聞かせる。
（6）TF 質問——すべてのパートに関する TF 質問（1 パート 5 問程度）が書かれたプリントを配布し，グループでのリテリングにおいて聞き取ったメモを参照しながら解答させる。解答の仕方については，T は本文の内容と同じ，F は本文の内容と異なる，NI（No Information）は他の生徒のリテリングでは発話されなかったものとする。グループで正解数を計算させ，どのグループが一番上手にリテリングをすることができたのかを競わせる。また，パートごとで一番得点の高い生徒も発表する。

自分のリテリングを録音している

録音したリテリングを聞いて振り返りをしている

## 8.2.3 研究の成果

### （1）スピーキング力の調査

6月（事前テスト）と1月（事後テスト）に実施したスピーキング課題の結果を表8-3にまとめます。ただし，どちらかを欠席した生徒は除外しました。分析方法としては，録音した発話を書き起こした40秒間での「発話語数」と「文の数」の平均値を産出しました。結果は表8-3にあるとおりです。

| | 事前テスト（6月） | 事後テスト（1月） |
|---|---|---|
| 発話語数 | 34.25（9.53） | 43.93（6.97） |
| 文の数 | 2.83（1.04） | 3.96（0.94） |

注）N = 76，平均（標準偏差）

**表8-3　スピーキング課題の結果**

統計分析の結果，事前テストと事後テストの発話語数の平均の差において，有意差は認められませんでしたが，効果量は大でした（有意差が認められるとは，誤差では済まされない差があったことを意味します）。また，文の数の平均の差において，1％水準での有意差が認められ，効果量は中でした。これらの結果から，ICレコーダーを活用した授業により，スピーキングにおける「流暢さ」が高まったことが示唆されました。

### （2）スピーキングに対する情意面の調査

「リテリング」と「即興的なスピーキング」に関する質問紙による調査結果を次ページの表8-4にまとめます。

統計分析の結果，質問項目1〜6の全てにおいて，1％水準での有意差が認められました。効果量は質問項目1〜5は中，質問項目6は小でした。これらの結果から，ICレコーダーを活用した授業は，リテリングや即興的なスピーキングに対する情意面に肯定的な影響を及ぼすことが示唆されました。

以下にリテリングについての意見調査（一部）を紹介します。

| 質問項目 | 6月 | 1月 |
|---|---|---|
| 1　リテリングを集中してできる。 | 3.88 (1.35) | 5.01 (1.13) |
| 2　リテリングを楽しみにしている。 | 2.84 (1.40) | 4.05 (1.22) |
| 3　リテリングでは「できた」という充実感が得られる。 | 3.14 (1.42) | 4.54 (1.31) |
| 4　即興的なスピーキングを集中してできる。 | 4.32 (1.40) | 5.09 (0.98) |
| 5　即興的なスピーキングを楽しみにしている。 | 3.16 (1.60) | 3.88 (1.43) |
| 6　即興的なスピーキングでは「できた」という充実感が得られる。 | 3.97 (1.56) | 4.47 (1.44) |

注）N = 76，平均（標準偏差）

表8-4　スピーキングに対する情意面の調査結果

●自分の力で要約してまとめるのが難しかった。何回も読むことで内容がよく分かったし，それを伝えるために伝え方の工夫を考えて実行することができてよかった。

●班ごとで TF の正解数を競い合うなど，楽しみながら活動ができた。理解だけでなく，他の人にそれを伝える力も向上した。リテリングはかなり難しかったが，それだけ力が付いたと思う。

●リテリングは相手に分かりやすくスピーキングをすることや相手のスピーキングの内容を聞き取る力が鍛えられると思いました。グループでの学習は個人とは違い，コミュニケーション力も向上するのでとても良いと思いました。

　以下に IC レコーダーについての意見調査（一部）を紹介します。

●自分の発話を振り返ることができるから，どこをどう改善したらよいのか分かりやすいので使うべき。

- 自分の発話を録音して聞くことができるので，発音の間違いなどが分かる。
- 自分の発話を録音できることで，発音や正しい表現を使えているかどうかを確認できるので，スピーキングの力は以前よりも向上したと思った。
- 私が一番いいなと思ったのは，自分で考えて話した英語が録音できて，それをまた聞けるという機能です。
- 教科書の音声を聞くときに，全体の授業では最後まで聞き終えないと2回目は聞けないが，IC レコーダーがあれば聞き取れなかったところまで自由に戻って聞くことができる。
- 自分のペースで音を聞けて，速度も変えられるので，英文が易しいときは速いスピードで聞いたり，逆に難しいときは遅い速度で聞いたりと，いろいろな使い方ができると思います。

### 8.2.4　この研究から見えてくる課題

　本研究では，IC レコーダーを用いて，一定期間リテリングを行うことで，生徒のスピーキング力が向上するのかについて，「流暢さ」に焦点を当てて検証しましたが，語彙や文法使用の誤りといった「正確さ」については検証していません。これは，「流暢さ」と「正確さ」はいわば「トレードオフ」の関係であることが主な理由です。つまり，「流暢さ」を求めれば求めるほど，誤りが多くなるという関係があるからです。しかし，「流暢さ」がある程度高まれば，「正確さ」も追及すべきなのは当然のことであり，この点が今後の課題であると考えています。

## 8.3　リテリングを日本語で行う効果についての研究

　本研究の目的は日本語によるリテリングが，英文筆記再生課題にどのような影響を与えるのかを日本語によるリテリングを行わない場合と比較検証することにより，生徒により適したリテリング指導を模索することです。英文筆記再生課題とは，読んだり，聞いたりした内容について，制限時間内に可能な限り書くものです。協力者は，公立高校の1年生1クラス（40名）です。本研究の研究課題は以下のとおりです。

〈研究課題〉

　英文筆記再生課題の前に日本語によるリテリングを行った場合（処置群）と日本語によるリテリングを行わなかった場合（対照群）を比較して，どちらが英文筆記再生課題における意味のまとまりであるアイデアユニット（以下，IU と略記）の得点が高いのか。また，どちらの総語数が多いのか。

## 8.3.1　先行研究

　Levelt（1989）は，第一言語の発話処理モデルを提案し，発話の心的処理を（1）「概念化装置（conceptualizer)」，（2）「形式化装置（formulator)」，（3）「調音装置（articulator)」という3つの段階に分類しています。（1）「概念化装置」は，「話したいことをまとめる段階」です。（2）「形式化装置」は，「話したいことをどのような語彙や文法を用いて表現するのかを決める段階」です。（3）「調音装置」は，「音韻情報を付加して，実際に音として発話する段階」です。本研究が対象とする本文の内容理解後に行うリテリングにおいても，上記モデル（1）〜（3）の段階を経ていると考え，日本語によるリテリングを取り入れることで，「概念化装置」の段階を強化でき，次に続く「形式化装置」の段階への移行がスムーズに行われるのではないかと考えました。

## 8.3.2　実験素材

　実験素材として，*LANDMARK English Communication I*（啓林館，平成25年度発行）の LESSON 6 The Doctor with the Hands of God の Part 2 と Part 4 を使用しました。実験素材の難易レベル等を次ページの表 8-5 に示します。

| | 難易<br>レベル | 単語数 | 文の数 | IU 数 | 1文における<br>語数の平均 |
|---|---|---|---|---|---|
| Part 2 | 8.8 | 94 | 6 | 18 | 15.6 |
| Part 4 | 8.4 | 89 | 6 | 18 | 14.8 |

（注）Microsoft Word 2007 を使用して，難易のレベルは Flesch-Kincaid Grade Levels で算出しました。

表8-5　実験素材のデータ

## 【本文プリント】

〈LESSON 6 Part 2〉

"Everything for the good of the patients" is Dr. Fukushima's motto. In order to do better operations, he invented the "keyhole" method. In traditional brain operations, doctors cut open a large area of the patient's skull, and that brings serious risk to the patient. The "keyhole" method reduces such risk and makes operations much more successful. The method requires only a small hole, about the size of a one-yen coin, on the patient's head. Through this "keyhole" and with the help of a surgical microscope, he can reach the tumor in the patient's brain.

「すべては患者のために」が福島医師のモットーです。よりよい手術を行うために，彼は「鍵穴」法を考案しました。従来の脳手術では，医師は患者の頭蓋骨（ずがいこつ）の大きな範囲を切り開きますが，そのことは患者に重大な危険をもたらします。「鍵穴」法はそのような危険を減らし，手術をさらにずっと成功させます。その方法では，患者の頭に1円硬貨ほどの大きさの小さな穴しか必要としません。この「鍵穴」を通して，外科用顕微鏡の助けを借りつつ，彼は患者の脳にある腫瘍にたどり着くことができるのです。

〈LESSON 6 Part 4〉

Today, as an experienced surgeon, Dr. Fukushima teaches his methods to students and younger doctors. One time, during an operation, a younger doctor made a mistake. As soon as Dr. Fukushima noticed it, he took the surgical knife away from the doctor. He then went on lecturing the doctor for six hours while he was correcting the mistake. When he sees younger doctors working too slow-ly, he always teaches them to work more quickly and carefully. He is a strict teacher but the younger doctors respect him very much.

　今日，経験豊かな外科医として，福島医師は学生や若手の医師に自分の手法を教えています。あるとき，手術中に若手の医師がミスを犯しました。福島医師はそれに気づくとすぐに，その医師から外科用メスを取り上げました。それから福島医師はミスを修正しながら，6時間その医師に説教し続けました。彼は若手の医師たちがあまりにもゆっくりと作業しているのを見ると，彼らにもっと迅速に注意深く作業するよう常に教えます。彼は厳しい教師ですが，若手の医師たちは彼をとても尊敬しています。

## 8.3.3　手順

　LESSON 6 の Part 2 を用いて，英文筆記再生課題を合計2回，LESSON 6 の Part 4 を用いて，日本語筆記再生課題を1回と英文筆記再生課題を1回，合計2回実施しました。ただし，本文プリントに日本語訳をつけることで，内容理解をすることが可能であると判断し，本文の解説プリントを提示しませんでした（解説プリントの違いが結果に影響することを避けたことも理由です）。また，音読指導も実施しませんでした。

| LESSON 6　Part 2 |

（1）本文プリント，英文筆記再生用紙1回目，2回目を裏向きで配布して，生徒には見ないように指示をする。
（2）本文プリントを表向きにして，本文を読ませる（語彙指導は事前に実施している）。メモをとらないことを指示する（3分間）。
（3）本文プリントを裏向きにするように指示をする。
（4）1回目と書かれた英文筆記再生用紙だけを表向きにして，指定されたキーワードを使って，英文筆記再生課題を行わせる（4分間）。
（5）1回目の英文筆記再生用紙を裏向けにするように指示する。
（6）2回目と書かれた英文筆記再生用紙を表向きにして，指定されたキーワードを使って，英文筆記再生課題を行わせる（4分間）。

（1）本文プリント，日本語筆記再生用紙，英文筆記再生用紙を裏向きで配布して，生徒には見ないように指示をする。

（2）本文プリントを表向きにして，本文を読ませる（語彙指導は事前に実施している）。日本語によるリテリングをしてから英語によるリテリングをする流れについては説明しない。また，メモをとらないことも指示する（3分間）。

（3）本文プリントを裏向きにするように指示をする。

（4）1回目と書かれた日本語筆記再生用紙だけを表向きにして，指定されたキーワードを使って，日本語筆記再生課題を行わせる（4分間）。

（5）日本語筆記再生用紙を裏向けにするように指示する。

（6）2回目と書かれた英文筆記再生用紙を表向きにして，指定されたキーワードを使って，英文筆記再生課題を行わせる（4分間）。

## 8.3.4　採点・分析方法

　採点基準として Ikeno（1996）の IU を使用し，テキスト情報がどのくらい再生されたのかを検証することとしましたが，記憶の影響を低くするために，手がかりとして本文で使用されているキーワードを提示しました。キーワードは 10 語以下の文は 1 語，11 語以上の文には 2 語を提示しました（Part 2 と Part 4 ともにキーワードは合計 12 個提示しました）。対象となる英文は合計 18 の IU に分割して分析を行いました。採点は全体の約 30%を 2 名の評価者（日本人英語教師とアメリカ人 AET）で行い，評価者間信頼係数は r = .96 であったので，残りの約 70%を日本人英語教師で採点しました。

〈誤りとしない〉

・冠詞の誤り

・単数と複数の誤り

・前置詞の誤り

・副詞がない

・時制の誤り

・綴りの誤り

・三人称単数 s のミス

**【IU の分割**（合計 18）**】** ※四角括弧は提示したキーワード

〈LESSON 6 Part 2〉

---

"① Everything for the good of the patients" / ② is Dr. Fukushima's motto. ③ In order to do better operations, / ④ he invented the "keyhole" method. ⑤ In traditional brain operations, / ⑥ doctors cut open a large area / ⑦ of the patient's skull, / ⑧ and that brings serious risk / ⑨ to the patient. ⑩ The "keyhole" method reduces such risk / ⑪ and makes operations much more successful. ⑫ The method requires only a small hole, / ⑬ about the size of a one-yen coin, / ⑭ on the patient's head. ⑮ Through this "keyhole" / ⑯ and with the help of a surgical microscope, / ⑰ he can reach the tumor / ⑱ in the patient's brain.

---

〈Lesson 6 Part 4〉

---

① Today, as an experienced surgeon, / ② Dr. Fukushima teaches his methods / ③ to students and younger doctors. ④ One time, / ⑤ during an operation, / ⑥ a younger doctor made a mistake. ⑦ As soon as Dr. Fukushima noticed it, / ⑧ he took the surgical knife away / ⑨ from the doctor. ⑩ He then went on lecturing the doctor / ⑪ for six hours / ⑫ while he was correcting the mistake. ⑬ When he sees younger doctors working too slowly, / ⑭ he always teaches them / ⑮ to work more quickly / ⑯ and carefully. ⑰ He is a strict teacher / ⑱ but the younger doctors respect him very much.

---

## 8.3.5　結果と考察

　英文筆記再生課題における「日→英」と「英→英」の IU の得点（合計 18 点）における記述統計を表 8-6 に示し，総語数における記述統計を表 8-7 に示します。「英→英」は 2 回目の英文筆記再生課題の結果を分析対象としました。

| | $n$ | 総得点平均（$SD$） | 差 |
|---|---|---|---|
| 日→英 | 39 | 10.46（3.32） | 5.77 |
| 英→英 | 39 | 4.69（2.44） | |

表8-6 「日→英」と「英→英」のIU得点における記述統計

| | $n$ | 総語数平均（$SD$） | 差 |
|---|---|---|---|
| 日→英 | 39 | 63.41（12.81） | 26.85 |
| 英→英 | 39 | 36.56（12.07） | |

表8-7 「日→英」と「英→英」の総語数における記述統計

　統計分析の結果，IU平均点の差と総語数平均の差の両方において，効果量は大であり，1％水準で有意差が認められました。このことにより，日本語によるリテリングが英文筆記再生課題に肯定的な影響を及ぼすことが示唆されました。

## 8.3.6　アンケート

　「日本語によるリテリングは有益であるか」という質問項目に対して自由記述で答えてもらいました。

**【肯定的な意見（一部）】36名**

○日本語が頭に残るから英語がスラスラ書けた。

○英語だけのリテリングは途中で何を言っているのか分からなくなるときがあるから，日本語でのリテリングを先にした方が英語でのリテリングがやりやすい。普段，リテリングをするときも，だいたいの日本語を要約してから英語を考えます。

○日本語でリテリングをする方が内容が整理されるので，パラフレーズがしやすかった。

○日本語にしてから英語にするのでより英文を思い出しやすい。

○日本語でリテリングをする方が英語でリテリングをするときに，書きた

いことが整理できて書きやすい。

○日本語でリテリングをする方が内容がまとまりやすい。

○日本語でリテリングをする方が話の内容が頭により残るのでリテリングがしやすかった。

○日本語でリテリングをする方が何を伝えればよいかがはっきり分かっているのでやりやすかった。

○日本語でリテリングをする方が文法を考えて書くことができました。

○日本語でのリテリングがあると，内容がよく頭に入って，後の英語が書きやすく，そのままの文ではなく，自分で文を考えたり，文法を使ったりして本文をリテリングすることができるから，日本語リテリングをやる方がよい。

**【否定的な意見（一部）】3名**

●日本語でのリテリングを入れても英語でのリテリングにはあまり関係ないように感じました。

●英語でリテリングをする方が自分のためになると思う。

## 第8章のまとめ

- ●リテリングを長期間行うことで，リテリングに対する動機が高まる。
- ●ICレコーダーを活用したリテリング活動を行うことで，スピーキングにおける「流暢さ」が向上することと，スピーキングに対する動機が高まる。
- ●「流暢さ」と「正確さ」は「トレードオフ」の関係であり，「流暢さ」を求めれば求めるほど，誤りが多くなる。
- ●第一言語の発話処理モデルでは，発話の心的処理を「概念化装置」，「形式化装置」，「調音装置」という3つの段階に分類している。「概念化装置」は，「話したいことをまとめる段階」であり，「形式化装置」は，「話したいことをどのような語彙や文法を用いて表現するのかを決める段階」であり，「調音装置」は，「音韻情報を付加して，実際に音として発話する段階」である。
- ●英語による筆記リテリングを行う前に，日本語による筆記リテリングを行わせると，それを行わない場合と比べて，意味のまとまりであるIUの数と総語数の両方において，伸びが見られる。

# おわりに

　本書では，検定教科書を使用したリテリング指導について解説をしました。指導する生徒の英語習熟度は様々ですが，たとえ上手に話せなくても，自分の言葉で他者に内容を伝える喜びを経験させる指導を追求してほしいと思います。英語を話すということは誤りが付きものですが，大切なのは，「英語を話したい！」，「伝えたい！」という気持ちです。そのような気持ちを育てるためには，日頃からアウトプットする活動を継続して行い，うまくいったこと，いかなかったことを振り返らせることが必要です。

　総合的な英語力は，植物を育てるときに必要となる水と栄養のように，「情熱」と「適切な指導」を与えることで，徐々に育ちます。本書を通して，「リテリング指導をやってみよう！」という「情熱」が沸き起こり，リテリング指導における「適切な指導」が教室での実践に繋がれば幸いです。

　本書の内容の多くは京都外国語大学大学院での著者の修士論文が元になっています。そのときの指導教官であった鈴木寿一先生（現在は桃山学院教育大学），杉本義美先生（京都外国語大学）には多くの貴重なご助言をいただきました。また，田地野彰先生（京都大学名誉教授，名古屋外国語大学）には意味順関連について貴重なご助言をいただきました。また，大修館書店の内田雅氏には，本書を執筆する機会をいただき，校正段階から完成まで的確なご助言をいただきました。この場を借りて厚くお礼申し上げます。

佐々木啓成

# 参考文献

池邊裕司（2004）.「Reproduction を用いた英語表現能力の育成」. *STEP Bulletin* 16 巻 146-152.

卯城祐司（2009）.『英語リーディングの科学—「読めたつもり」の謎を解く』. 研究社.

甲斐あかり（2008）.「英文読解テストとしての再話課題の有効性の検証：テキストタイプ，産出言語，採点方法の妥当性を中心として」. *STEP Bulletin* 20 巻 76-94.

加藤澄恵（2012）.「学習活動が英語学習者の内発的動機に与える影響の検証」.『言語文化論叢』第 6 号 9 -22. 千葉大学言語教育センター.

門田修平（2012）.『シャドーイング・音読と英語習得の科学』. コスモピア.

小泉利恵（2016）.「ルーブリックを使ったスピーキングの評価」.『英語教育』12 月号，34-35. 大修館書店.

ジャパンライム株式会社（2017）.「ラウンド制指導法実践マニュアル高等学校におけるラウンド制指導」.

静哲人（2002）.『英語テスト作成の達人マニュアル』. 大修館書店.

鈴木寿一（2005）. 英語教育理論と実践の融合：基礎力が不十分な学生の英語力を引き上げるには　第 50 回関西英語英米文学会講演　西宮：関西学院大学

田地野彰（2011）.『「意味順」英語学習法』. ディスカヴァー・トゥエンティンワン.

西巌弘（2010）.『即興で話す英語力を鍛える！ワードカウンターを活用した驚異のスピーキング活動 22』. 明治図書.

ベネッセ教育総合研究所（2015）.「中高の英語指導に関する実態調査 2015」.

村野井仁（2006）. 『第二言語習得研究から見た効果的な英語学習法・指導法』. 大修館書店.

文部科学省（2018）. 「平成 29 年度　英語教育改善のための英語力調査事業報告」.

山本良一（1998）. 「総合英語の中で話す力を伸ばす」. 『英語教育』 9 月号, 17-19. 大修館書店.

Alderson, J. C.（2000）. *Assessing reading.* Cambridge University Press.

Ikeno, O.（1996）. The effects of text-structure-guiding questions on comprehension of texts with varying linguistic difficulties. *JACET Bulletin*, 27, 51-68.

Irwin, P. A., & Mitchell. J. N.（1983）. A procedure for assessing the richness of retellings. *Journal of Reading*, 26, 391-396.

Kai, A.（2009）. Achieving Global Coherence Through Retelling. *Annual Review of English Language Education in Japan*, 20, 41-50.

Kai, A.（2011）. Comparison of Two Post-Reading Tasks: Retelling vs. Recall. *Annual Review of English Language Education in Japan*, 22, 249-264.

Lee, J. F.（1986）. On the use of recall task to measure L2 reading comprehension. *TESOL Quartely*, 13, 565-572.

Levelt, W. J. M.（1989）. *Speaking: From intention to articulation.* Cambridge, MA:MIT Press.

Ryan, R. M., & Deci, E. L.（2002）. Overview of self-determination theory: An organismic dialectical perspective. In E. L. Deci, & R. M. Ryan （Eds.）, *Handbook of self-determination research*（pp. 3 -33）. Rochester, NY: University of Rochester Press.

Swain, M.（2005）. The output hypothesis: Theory and research. In E. Hinkel（Ed.）, *Handbook of research in second language teaching and learning*（pp.471-483）. Mahwah: Lawrence Erlbaum Associates.

Yokouchi, Y.（2014）. Comparative Study of the Characteristics of Utterances in Retelling Tasks: Case of Text Length, Difficulty, and Input Mode. *JACET-KANTO Journal* Vol. 1, 64-79.

## [著者紹介]

### 佐々木啓成 （ささき　よしなり）

京都外国語大学大学院外国語学研究科博士前期課程修了。現在，京都府立鳥羽高等学校教諭。平成22年度京都府現職教育職員長期研修の派遣教員として，京都大学高等教育研究開発推進センターにて研修。平成26年度若手英語教員米国派遣交流事業の派遣教員として，アイオワ州立大学にて研修。平成30年度パナソニック教育財団実践研究助成指定校代表研究者。2018年第68回全国英語教育研究大会（全英連滋賀大会）高等学校分科会の発表者。検定教科書では，*LANDMARK Fit English Communication I, II, III*（共著：新興出版社啓林館），*Revised Vision Quest English Expression I Standard*（編集協力者：新興出版社啓林館）。著書には，『「意味順」で中学英語をやり直す本』（共著：KADOKAWA/中経出版，2012），*A New Approach to English Pedagogical Grammar: The Order of Meanings*（共著：Routledge, UK, 2018）がある。大学入試関連では，『「意味順」でつくる英語をたのしむ vol. 1, 2, 3』（ラーンズ），『大学入試長文シリーズ Front Runner 2, 4』（数研出版）を執筆。英語指導 DVD では，『「ラウンド制指導法実践マニュアル」高等学校におけるラウンド制指導』（ジャパンライム）の授業者。また，全国英語教育学会や外国語教育メディア学会において発表経験あり。

リテリングを活用した英語指導——理解した内容を自分の言葉で発信する

© SASAKI Yoshinari, 2020　　　　　　　　　　　　　NDC375／viii, 150p／21cm

初版第1刷──2020年9月1日
　第3刷──2022年3月20日

著者────────佐々木啓成
発行者───────鈴木一行
発行所───────株式会社 大修館書店
　　　　　　　　　〒113-8541 東京都文京区湯島2-1-1
　　　　　　　　　電話03-3868-2651（販売部）　03-3868-2292（編集部）
　　　　　　　　　振替00190-7-40504
　　　　　　　　　［出版情報］https://www.taishukan.co.jp

装丁────────CCK
印刷所───────広研印刷
製本所───────ブロケード

ISBN978-4-469-24643-8　Printed in Japan